WORLD WAR II CONSCIENTIOUS OBJECTORS
GERMFASK, MICHIGAN,
THE ALCATRAZ CAMP

Jane Kopecky

Editor: Tyler Tichelaar
Layout: Stacey Willey, Globe Printing, Ishpeming MI
Cover Art: Michelle Earle
Technical Assistance: Susanne Barr

Every attempt has been made to source properly all quotes.
Printed in the United States of America

"Civilian Public Service Camp 135 at Germfask, Michigan, is "a bubbling cauldron," whose story needs to be told."

~ Harry R. Van Dyck, author of *Exercise of Conscience: A WWII Objector Remembers,*

"Here Jane Kopecky reveals the nearly-forgotten story of Camp Germask, where some of the most ardent war-resisters among World War II conscientious objectors were held for 13 months in 1944 and 1945. Opponents of the war and conscription on a variety of religious, pacifist, or political grounds, these recalcitrant dissenters dared imprisonment as they refused to cooperate with rules of the Selective Service. Instead of jail, they ended up in what some of them called the Alcatraz of CO camps and their sympathizers elsewhere in the country called "America's Siberia." In interview transcripts, memoirs, and documents collected by Jane Kopecky, their lives and their relations with their Germfask and other Upper Peninsula neighbors come alive. This book is a great read and a great service to historical understanding."

~ Howard Brick, Louis Evans Professor of History, University of Michigan

"The primary sources on the CPS camp at Germfask, Michigan, have historical value. Jane Kopecky is to be commended for making them accessible to the reading public through her book."

~ Will Underwood, Acquiring Editor, *The Kent State University Press*

"Before the Vietnam War, being a conscientious objector was equivalent to being a criminal in this country. In this new book, Jane Kopecky sheds much needed light on the little known conscientious objectors camp at Germfask, Michigan, during World War II, how the local community responded to the camp, and how America has changed its opinion of conscientious objectors since then. Thank you, Jane, for returning to us this invaluable piece of our American heritage--it's a story that has been left out of the limelight for far too long."

~ Tyler Tichelaar, PhD, Award-Winning Author of *Iron Pioneers* and *When Teddy Came to Town*

"Many people know that World War II conscientious objectors were assigned to civilian service to care for patients in mental hospitals, to work in national parks or to jump out of airplanes to fight forest fires. But few know about the men who refused to do any alternative service at all. They were sent to a work camp in the virtual wilderness of Michigan's Upper Peninsula. In this book, Jane Kopecky tells their fascinating story – why they were sent to Germfask, how they survived, and how the locals treated them."

~ Marcus D. Rosenbaum, Former senior editor, *NPR*

To my mother, Dorothy Lee,
and my grandfather, Raymond Hastings

ACKNOWLEDGMENTS

I wish to thank the following people and organizations for their contributions to this book:

My family for their support and encouragement. My daughter Susanne for editing pictures

The following for additional editing suggestions: Vonciel LeDuc, Professor Howard Brick, University of Michigan, and Will Underwood, the Kent State University Press

Stacey Willey of Globe Printing for her guidance and getting the book into publication

Marcus Rosenbaum and National Public Radio

The Seney National Wildlife Refuge staff

The Escanaba Daily Press

Big Cedar Campground

The Manistique Public Library staff

And especially, all the people and families who consented to be interviewed or shared their memories, letters, and pictures for inclusion in this book.

A Note on the Text

Original documents were used throughout this book. They have not been altered other than to update or modernize spelling, correct punctuation, write out abbreviations for clarity, or correct errors in the original so the flow of a sentence will be easier for the reader to understand. In no case have they been altered to change the intention of the writer or speaker. Most of these documents are in the possession of the author, unless otherwise noted.

CONTENTS

PREFACE

Little is known about the 151 conscientious objector camps regulated by the Selective Service System that were located throughout the United States during World War II. Even less is known about a camp in Germfask, Michigan, where the most troublesome political dissidents were relocated. The Selective Service supposedly sent these men to Germfask to work at the Seney National Refuge under the direction of the Mennonite Church, but that was a guise. **Official documents reveal, "This unit was set up in cooperation with the Michigan State Board of Mental Hygiene to make observations and study of noncooperative objectors who were believed to be mentally and physically deficient."** [1]

Selective Service personnel knew the conscientious objectors (COs) would be unwilling workers. Their goal was to isolate them, study their behavior, and keep them out of the public eye until it could determine what to do with them. The paid employees in charge of the camp were unsuspecting, uninformed, and unprepared for the job they were about to undertake. They expected the COs would be religious men with strong work ethics. But, they learned quickly the conscientious objectors' convictions were strong against the war and that many detested being in Civilian Public Service, which they called American-style concentrations camps. Some did not want to be any part of the system. They turned the lives of government employees into a living nightmare. With the exception of four men the employee turnover at the camp was high. One man worked only one half day.

Placing all the "bad boys" in one camp gave the COs the opportunity to discuss and to strategize how they could intensify their objections to war and conscription. Their Mahatma Gandhi style of nonviolent protests, and their battles with the legal system and the government, sometimes became front page headlines for major newspapers across the country. The camp became notorious. The word "Germfask" became the symbol for World War II protesters. It was called the Alcatraz of all camps-the last stop before prison. The struggles, tensions, and confrontations that occurred in

1   Selective Service System. *Conscientious Objection: Special Monograph.* Vol I. No. 11. Washington, DC: Government Printing Office, 1950. p. 234.

this remote Northern Michigan village became an idealistic conflict between conscientious objectors and a country in support of the war. Today, however, few people know about these World War II conscientious objectors, and only a handful realize that Germfask, Michigan became a center for non-violent resistance. Most of the local residents are unaware of this part of their community's history.

PART I

GERMFASK—WHAT AN UNUSUAL NAME

Germfask is located in the east central part of Michigan's Upper Peninsula in the northern part of Schoolcraft County about halfway between Lake Superior and Lake Michigan. It is bordered on the north, west, and south by 95,238 acres of the Seney National Wildlife Refuge and on the east by the Manistique River. It was settled in 1866 during the heyday of the big lumber era. It was originally called the "The Dump," a logging term, because logs were dumped on the riverbank until spring break-up. When the ice melted, the logs were floated down river to a natural harbor in Manistique on the shores of Lake Michigan. At Manistique, the logs were sawed into lumber at one of the three mills, then shipped by barge across Lake Michigan to Chicago or other large industrial areas.

In 1882, local residents met to decide on an official town name. One of the men proposed using the first initial of each of the original settlers' surnames, as follows:

Grant, John,

Edge, Matthew

Robinson, George

Mead, Thaddeus

French, Dr. W. W.

Ackley, Ezekiel

Shepard, Oscar

Knaggs, Hezekiah

Thus, the name was changed from The Dump to Germfask.[2]

THE GERMFASK-SENEY REFUGE CONNECTION

State highway M77 runs through Germfask. Six miles to the north is Seney, a once-notorious logging village. Seney began as a settlement about 1881 as a train stop for passengers who wanted to travel a footpath to Grand Marais, Michigan, a harbor town on the shores of Lake Superior, twenty-five miles to the north. In 1882, the Alger, Smith Company and other logging companies moved in to begin clear-cutting thousands of square miles of virgin white pine from the Seney Plains and surrounding areas. Cutting the pine required a large workforce, and immigrants arrived by the railcar-load to work for one dollar a day and their room and board, a standard wage at that time. Seney suddenly changed from a train stop to a thriving town of approximately 3,000 people. On weekends, its population swelled even larger as lumberjacks arrived from the fifteen or so nearby logging camps.[3]

When the big pine was cut, the timber companies and migrant lumberjacks moved to other areas, leaving behind thousands of acres of barren land. Seney then changed from a roaring lumber town to a small village.

About 1908, some Schoolcraft County residents formed a group to advertise cheap real estate and encourage settlement in the Upper Peninsula. Real estate in the Upper Peninsula was selling for five to twenty-five dollars per acre compared to one-hundred to two-hundred dollars per acre in places like Illinois and Indiana.

A land investment syndicate called Western Land and Surety Company paid one dollar per acre for thousands of acres in the Seney area. It planned to drain the marshes and sell them as farmland. However, the investors were not aware the marshy sand-covered peat soils were not suitable for crops, so the venture failed.

The families who purchased the land had been scammed. For example, a colony of Jews settled there and nearly starved to death during a brutal winter. Fortunately, the citizens of nearby Newberry came to their aid. Newspapers labeled the venture "The Great Land Swindle."[4]

The Seney Marshes, unsuitable for farming, were an excellent environ-

3   Holbrook, Stewart H. *Holy Old Mackinaw: A Natural History of the American Lumberjack.* New York: Macmillan, 1938.
4   *Detroit News.* January 10, 1911.

ment for migratory birds. In 1935, the United States Fish and Wildlife Service purchased the Seney Marshes and turned them into a refuge and breeding ground for birds and other wildlife. Roads, dikes, ditches, and dams were laid out and constructed throughout the refuge. Men from the Civilian Conservation Core (CCC) built dorms on the south end of town and lived in them while working on the refuge's various projects. Their work continued on the refuge until World War II when all eligible young men were drafted by Selective Service.

When the conscientious objectors arrived in Germfask in 1944, they entered a village isolated both physically and socially. The nearest "large" towns (with populations of about 6,000 at the time) were Manistique and Newberry, both forty miles away. Many residents were descendants of the original settlers and everyone was on a first-name basis. Neighbors united in times of disaster to assist those in need.

The Seney National Wildlife Refuge and the Upper Peninsula Hospital for the Insane in Newberry offered stable employment to some and many worked in the local timber industry. Families often supplemented their incomes by raising livestock for slaughter, milking the family cow and selling the cream, growing their own gardens, and hunting and trapping wild game. They were independent with a strong sense of work ethics. When World War II broke out, their young men answered the call, some would never return.

THE GENESIS OF THIS BOOK

Main Street looking South about 1940

I grew up in the 1940s and 1950s on a small farm twelve miles south of Germfask. We had no phone and no car. The nearest neighbor was a quarter-mile away. Seeing strangers was a nearly unheard of occasion that brought excitement and sometimes a sense of danger.

One of my earliest memories is from the spring of 1945. My sister and I were playing on the front porch of our farmhouse. Three strangers emerged from a nearby wooded area and walked across the field toward our house. Mom came out, pointed to the men, and told us, "Come inside right now; hurry!"

Mom took our hands and walked us into the living room toward a door that opened to our front yard. She was trembling with fear for our safety. We were going to run to our neighbors' house but as she began to open the door, she realized the men were too near for us to make a safe break. She brought us back into the kitchen. She looked out the window again, then said, "No matter what happens, don't let those men in; don't open the door."

I was very young, but I sensed the danger. Mom was scared, and because she was scared, I became terrified. I stood in the middle of the kitchen floor and screamed and cried. Mom placed two kitchen chairs next to the window so my sister and I could look out. That calmed me. The three of us watched as the men came closer. They did not attempt to break into our house; instead, they stopped at a stone pile about one hundred feet from our front door. Over the years, those stones had been hand-picked from our fields and conveniently tossed near the barnyard gate.

A man wearing a funny cap picked up a stone. He pointed at it and then passed it to the next man. They discussed it for a long time before putting it into a gunnysack. They seemed oblivious to everything around them, totally immersed with the stones. My fear faded and I became curious. Some of the stones they put back onto the rock pile. Others went into the sack. This activity continued for a while.

The man in the funny hat looked toward the house. He glanced at the window and saw us looking back at him. Then he continued talking with the other two men and we continued watching. Several times, he looked toward us.

A short time later, a car turned onto our road. My mother rushed out the side door and flagged our neighbor to stop. She pointed to the men in our barnyard. The neighbor immediately jumped out of the car and ran over to them. After he said something in a gruff voice, they picked up the gunnysack and walked toward the road. A few minutes later, they were out of our sight.

That evening when Dad heard about the incident, he was very upset. He loaded the gun and said to Mom, "If those men from Germfask come close to the house, use the gun. Why are they allowed to roam around the country? I should slash that minister's car tires. He brought them here."

As the years went by, the summer of 1945 faded in my memory, but those events remained etched there, mysteries in search of a solution. In time, I found the answers to all those questions. Thirty-four years later, I actually spoke and corresponded with the man who was in our barnyard that day, the one in the funny hat who was so interested in a pile of farm field rocks. I discovered, in my own backyard, a sliver of American history that had never been recorded, a story that resonated back to the earliest days of our nation and forward to the 1960s and beyond—the story of Camp 135 and the incorrigible objectors of World War II.

LOCAL INTERVIEWS

It wasn't until 1979, when I was taking a graduate history class at Northern Michigan University and working on an oral history project that my memories about the Germfask camp resurfaced. I asked my neighbors whether they knew anything about the "Germfask Men."

They did. Or at least thought they did.

"Oh, you mean the conchies," one said. "We all called them conchies." ("Conchie" is short for "conscientious objector.")

"They were cowards," said another. "They said they didn't believe in killing, but do you think anyone who fought in that war liked killing? They had a job to do, but the conchies were too scared to do it."

"They thought they were better than us," a third told me.

And another: "Some of them were communists."

And another: "Someone paid Osborne, the Mennonite minister, to take care of them. Something to do with the church."

"I remember them," said one. "Rich families paid off government officials to keep their son's out of the war. They sent them to Germfask because we're so far in the boonies no one could find them. They'd walk to the post office and open their letters, then flash the money they were mailed."

"One of them raped a girl in Newberry," another revealed. "When they came back the next Saturday night, a group of men were waiting to lynch him. They chased him through the back streets, and just as they were about to catch him, the Germfask camp truck came by. His buddies pulled him into the truck while it was still going. He escaped. None of them came back to town again."

NEIGHBOR

I arrived unannounced at my elderly neighbor's house. She was on her porch peacefully rocking in her chair as we greeted each other. When I asked her whether she remembered the conscientious objectors, she stopped rocking. Her hands moved from a relaxed position on her lap to a tight grasp at the end of the armrest. She leaned forward in the chair and stared at me. We sat in silence for a few seconds. I was surprised by her reaction. My question had angered her.

She took a deep breath and, with complete disgust in her voice, she said, "Oh, yes, I remember them. They wanted to play a game of baseball. Well, the war was on, and the older boys and young men were fighting for our country. My son got a team together to play against them. It wasn't fair. Our team had only young boys who weren't starting to fill out in the shoulders. Those conchies were grown men. Our boys didn't have a chance. You should have heard the crowd hollering. The crowd was quite angry, so the umpire had to cancel the game. Those conchies left in a hurry. They shouldn't have been playing ball against our boys that Sunday. They should have been out with the men fighting a war." She angrily slapped her right hand on the armrest as she finished. "That was the first and last game they ever played against any of our local boys."

Her phone rang and she waved "goodbye." To my great surprise, when I returned the following day, she did not want to continue our conversation. When I asked her specific questions about the ball game, she pretended she hadn't told me about it. She said, "I don't really recall much about them".

INTIMIDATED

When I asked another neighbor about the conscientious objectors and a possible planned lynching, he folded his arms across his chest and squinted his eyes. In a menacing voice, he said, "I don't know nothing." That was the end of that conversation.

ANONYMOUS NEIGHBOR

When I asked another neighbor whether he remembered the camp, he stared at me for a few seconds with an embarrassed look. Then he got a little red in the face and said, "I'll tell you, but don't use my name. It was a Saturday night. A group of us high school boys had a few beers and we drove into the camp. We wanted to see just what was going on there. We were going to stir things up a little bit. No one was around, not one person; it was really weird. I got out of the car and shit on the front steps, and then we drove the hell out."

ED KORENICH

Ed Korenich owned the Jolly Inn Bar in Germfask. When I interviewed him in 1985, he told me:

"The first week they arrived, a couple of them came into the bar late in the evening and ordered beer. I served them once, then told them when they finished I'd prefer they not come back. They were polite. I didn't have anything against them, but I knew if they came back there'd be trouble."

MARTHA SHEPARD

Martha Shepard was a young Mennonite girl during the time the COs were at Germfask.

"A few of them came to church once in a while. They must have walked from Germfask because no local person would have given them a ride. It was quite a walk, about four miles. They were rich. Two of them had fathers who were lawyers. One was from Chicago and the other one was from way out west somewhere. We were afraid to talk with them."

BETTY

Betty attended the local high school during the war.

Betty: Our families worked hard for very little money, but they [the conscientious objectors] refused to work and lived the life of luxury.

Jane: What do you mean, they refused to work? What work?

Betty: They were supposed to be working at the refuge, but they wouldn't work. My friend's dad was one of the men in charge of them. He was the only man who did get them to work.

Jane: How did he do it?

Betty: I was told he carried a gun, and he told them he'd shoot them if they didn't.

Jane: But how could he do that? How could he get away with it?

Betty: He just did; nobody cared. They gang-raped a girl in Newberry. It was all covered up. They could get away with anything.

Jane: Did you ever talk with any of them?

Betty: No, I don't think anyone did. You could talk to Bruce Handrich, he was in that camp.

PASSAGE OF THE CONSCRIPTION BILL

In 1939, Germany aggressively began its march in conquest of Europe and World War II began. Realizing the United States could be drawn into war, Americans were debating isolationism and intervention. Three religious sects, the Mennonites, the Society of Friends (Quakers), and the Brethren, commonly referred to as the Peace Churches, actively encourage their members not to participate in war. While the government debated the Selective Service Act, and prior to its enactment, the Peace Churches and other pacifist organizations worked together and formed the National Interreligious Service Board for Conscientious Objectors (NISBCO).[5] They vigorously lobbied Congress to keep their members from participating in war in any form and stressed the importance of their nonviolent beliefs. They told about the cruel treatment conscientious objectors had endured in previous wars.[6]

During World War I, pacifists could either join the military or go to jail. Some objectors were sentenced to prison for as long as twenty years where daily beatings were reported. Some died there as a result of their treatment. Those who were drafted and placed in military camps were harassed and sometimes tortured. At an army camp in the state of Washington, two Mennonite men who were conscientious objectors worked in the mess hall. They were not required to wear army uniforms since it was against their belief. They were harassed during the day by fellow servicemen, but they were tortured at night after the lights went out. They were often pulled out of their bunks and forced to stand while insults were hurled at them. They were not allowed to sleep for more than a few hours. The harassment intensified. They were forced to walk or run outside around the camp's perimeters. Finally, the game turned deadly. They were forced to run while a man chased them on a motorcycle as a crowd cheered. One night, the motorcycle ran over one of the men, killing him. Cause of death was listed as accidental and the case was closed.[7]

5   National Service Board for Religious Objectors, bulletin, *The Origins of Civilian Public Service*, 1941.
6   Van Dyck, Harry R., Exercise of Conscience. Prometheus Books, Buffalo, New York, 1990.
7   National Service Board for Religious Objectors, bulletin, The Origins of Civilian Public Service, 1941.

The Peace Churches' lobbying was successful. The Selective Training and Service Act (Burke-Wadsworth Bill) was signed on September 16, 1940. It authorized the first-peace time draft of all eligible men and was the first time Congress fully recognized and made allowances for conscientious objectors. President Roosevelt reluctantly and with great reservations signed the bill.

Conscientious objectors opposed to combatant duty were now removed entirely from the military system. The bill included a IV-E classification to any man who "by reason of religious training and belief, is conscientiously opposed to participation in war in any form…in lieu of such induction, be assigned to work of national importance under civilian direction."[8] General Lewis B. Hershey, Director of Selective Service, believed, "Every draftee was to serve in some capacity, and duty-bound to serve their nation.[9] "

Statistically, the small number of conscientious objectors did not have an adverse effect on military manpower procurement or the war effort. Of the more than ten million Americans inducted during World War II, approximately 12,000 requested IV-E classification, another 6,000 were jailed, and roughly 22,000 opted to be inducted into the armed forces for noncombatant service for whatever purpose they were needed.[10]

But what to do with these men? When the bill was signed neither the work of national importance nor the mechanics of how to implement it had been determined. Several plans were formulated, but none were approved, the major stumbling block being money.[11]

8   *Selective Service System, Conscientious Objection: Special Monograph.* Vol I. No. 11. Washington, DC: Government Printing Office, 1950. p. 86-87.
9   Burke-Wadsworth Bill, the Selective Service and Training Act of 1940.
10 *National Interreligious Service Board for Conscientious Objectors.* Revised. Washington, DC: Director of Civilian Public Service, 1996. p. ii.
11 Keim, Albert N. *The CPS Story: An Illustrated History of Civilian Public Service.* Intercourse, PA: Good Books, 1990. p. 28-29.

ORGANIZING CIVILIAN PUBLIC SERVICE (CPS)

The Civilian Conservation Corps (CCC) had been organized in 1933, during the Great Depression, to decrease unemployment and promote worthwhile conservation programs that would benefit the entire nation. It was a successful and popular program being phased out in 1940 because of the conscription of young men and the war-time economy reducing unemployment. The federal agencies that had sponsored the CCC—the Forest Service, Soil Conservation Service, National Park Service, and the Department of Agriculture and Reclamation—now needed manpower for their projects and the churches needed suitable projects for their members. A mutually beneficial plan had been found. Men classified IV-E would continue the work of the CCC. The program would be called Civilian Public Service (CPS).[12]

All camps would be under the control of General Lewis Hershey, head of the Selective Service System and, through him, more directly by a Colonel Kosch. CPS had its own set of rules that did not follow the protocol of the armed forces. The CPS camp director, a member of a Peace Church, would be responsible for the behavior of the men.

The churches assumed the government would bear the brunt of the financial responsibility for CPS programs since the men would be engaged in government service. Now that the plan was formalized, Selective Service informed the churches they would have to finance everything or go along with a completely government-administered program. Many COs declared they wanted to serve under the religious agencies. The churches were determined to keep their men out of the control of the military. Orie Miller spoke for most Mennonites when he said, "Mennonites would gladly pay their share of the bill. They would do it even though every Mennonite farmer had to mortgage his farm." Meanwhile, the Society of Friends approved a resolution that if government funds became available they would not be accepted. The churches decided to attempt administration of the program on an experimental basis.[13]

12   Selective Service System. *Conscientious Objection: Special Monograph.* Vol I. No. 11. Washington, DC: Government Printing Office, 1950. p. 157-180.
13   Ibid. p.30.

Under the agreement, the churches paid the government thirty-five dollars per month for every man in camp. The men would not receive wages and their families would not receive government assistance in any form. The churches had to furnish medical expenses, clothing, the men's finances, and whatever else the government required. They also supplied each man an allowance of between $2.50 and $5.00 a month for personal needs. This put the churches under a financial strain. Members held work bees to can food and sew clothing that they delivered to the camps. They pooled their money to support families who couldn't afford the monthly payments.[14]

Service-without-pay caused feelings of exasperation and distress among some of the COs. Danny Dingman, whose memoir is included later in this book, states, "Although Congress had provided for conscientious objectors to be paid at the same rate as privates in the army, Hershey and Kosch never requested the money in their appropriations and drafted conscientious objectors never received any pay. This was undoubtedly partly due to the overzealousness of the churches, which volunteered to run the camps as a testimony to their faith(s). The church camp officials then "requested" that assignees contribute $35, —in addition to providing their own clothing, toiletries, etc."

The federal government allowed conscientious objectors to use vacated CCC camps for housing, and the federal agencies supplied the work, fifty-two hours a week, five-and-a-half days a week. [15]

The first CPS camp was in Grottoes, Virginia. The Mennonites were in charge of this camp and had to spend a substantial amount of money on repairs. They expressed concern about having to renovate the camp, after which Selective Service agreed to furnish camps in good condition and to maintain and repair them. Between 1941 and 1946, 151 CPS camps were established throughout the United States, housing 11,950 men.[16] When a camp became full, another one would be opened. For the most part, the camps served their intended purpose. (Appendix A – Camp Locations)

14   Hershberger, Guy, Franklin. The Mennonite Church in the Second World War. Scottdale, Pa: Mennonite Publishing House, 1951. p.70.
15   Selective Service System. *Conscientious Objection: Special Monograph*. Vol I. No. 11. Washington, DC: Government Printing Office, 1950. p. 191-207.
16   National Interreligious Service Board For Conscientious Objectors. Directory of CPS. Scottdale, PA: Mennonite Publishing House, 1996.

Below is a list of what the COs were instructed to bring to camp.[17]

WHAT TO BRING TO CAMP
From Instructions Sent to Each Camper

1. Not more than one suit of clothes suitable for Sunday wear.
2. Not more than one camp suit; these clothes suitable for wear evenings and Saturdays.
3. Overcoat.
4. Raincoat
5. Work Clothes:
    a. Three pairs of good quality blue denim trousers.
    b. Three good quality work shirts.
    c. Three good quality blue denim jackets
    d. Light sweater or similar windbreaker garment to wear under jacket when necessary.
    e. Two pairs of gloves.
    f. Two good pairs of work shoes.
    g. One pair of overshoes (arctics).
    h. One warm cap.
    i. Six pairs of work socks.
6. Three shirts for good wear.
7. One pair of good business shoes.
8. Several pairs of Sunday socks.
9. Underwear:
    a. Two pairs medium weight long underwear with long sleeves and legs.
    b. Lighter underwear if desired for camp purposes.
10. Two pairs of pajamas.
11. Linens:
    a. Three sheets good quality; at least 63 by 99 inches when finished.
    b Two pillow cases, same quality material.
    c. Three hand towels.
    d. Two bath towels.
    e. Two wash cloths.
12. Personal items - supplies may later be replenished in camp:
    a. Shaving supplies.
    b. Dental supplies.
    c. Toilet supplies
    d. Shoe polish supplies.
    e. Stationary and stamps.
    f. Literature supplies – notebook, devotional literature, Bible, etc.
    g. Musical instrument if desired.
    h. Hand mirror.
    i. Mending kit, needles, thread, pins, buttons, etc.
    j. Other personal items that you consider indispensable.

Do not bring a whole wardrobe, that is too many supplies. They will be a burden to you in camp. This clothing need NOT BE NEW, but can be supplied from your present wardrobe; the above list is to guide you as to quantity and quality.

17   Keim, Albert N. *The CPS Story: An illustrated History of Civilian Public Service.* Intercourse, PA: Good Books, 1990. p. 29.

CARLTON HOLLISTER
Author interview, May, 1980, Manistique, Michigan

This serves as an example of a CO who opted to serve in church sponsored camps.

"I was born in 1915 and raised in the Methodist Church doctrine. I was a farm boy and, by nature, not too aggressive. I preferred to settle differences peaceably. I don't ever remember being in a fight.

"At the age of fourteen, I saw the movie *All Quiet on the Western Front* and vowed never to participate in war. Naturally, I hoped there would never be another one.

"During high school, I developed a desire to be a forester, and after graduation in 1934, I entered Michigan State University. After being accepted by the university, I found out that among the required courses were two years of ROTC. I decided to participate as required in order to get the forestry training. The first two years were basic, and no commitment to the military was officially required; however, at the beginning of the second year, all students who were determined not to take advanced ROTC courses were asked to identify themselves. I stated I would not take advanced courses, to the disgust of my classmates. I knew my instructors would hold a grudge against me for my decision so I would no longer receive high grades even if I earned them. I did not regret my decision because I was assigned as equipment operator more than as leader of personnel.

"My ROTC experience increased my determination never to participate in war or the military in any form. The whole emphasis seemed to be based on submission of one's will to that of an officer whose object was to destroy whoever was declared an enemy at that particular time or to destroy the lives and property of someone else as he decided.

"I graduated from MSU in May of 1939 and began working as a ranger in a state park for the State of Michigan. On October 19, 1940, I registered with Selective Service as required by law. In the early winter of 1940, I received a questionnaire from the draft board. I made out the proper forms, applying for consideration as one who is conscientiously opposed to participation in combat in any form because of religious training and belief. Attached to this form was a statement from the Methodist Church stating the support it would give to one of its members who held such convictions. I also included names of references who were acquainted with my past behavior, character, and life standards.

"On July 24, 1941, I was mailed an order to report for work of national importance under Civilian direction at a camp in Manistee, Michigan, operated by the Church of the Brethren. When I arrived, I found about fifteen men living in tents on a farm. We were later moved to an abandoned CCC camp that was officially named CPS #117. The money to support this camp was contributed by the Brethren churches throughout the country. Some assignees worked at camp operation and maintenance while the balance of the men were assigned to the technical agency for which the camp was established.

"In our spare time, we did whatever we could to help the community—firefighting, barn building, or any service they needed. There was a shortage of manpower at that time, and we felt we were doing a valuable service. It was difficult to walk down the street and know that you were tolerated, but you would never be accepted.

Mrs. Hollister: I was scared. I heard about the wife of a conscientious objector who was seriously burned. She was just walking along the street when a local woman came out from her house and deliberately threw hot cooking grease onto her face. News spread quickly through the CPS camps about what had happened. It was a difficult time, but I was proud of Carlton. I supported his decision.

SELECTIVE SERVICE CAMPS

Because the churches had to accept all men classified as conscientious objectors, the church camps became a "holding tank" for those few men who refused to cooperate with the system.[18] As time progressed, the Selective Service System decided to finance a camp to segregate the "problem-type assignees." In addition, some religious objectors opted to go to the Selective Service camps so they would not be a financial burden to their families or the church. Unlike the church-sponsored camps, the Selective Service Camps (SSS) eliminated the $35 a month fee, supplied clothing and food, and gave each man a $5 monthly allowance.

The first SSS camp was opened in July of 1943 at Mancos, Colorado. When the Mancos camp became full, the most uncooperative men were identified and sent to the second SSS camp in La Pine, Oregon.

18   Selective Service System. *Conscientious Objection: Special Monograph.* Vol I. No. 11. Washington, DC: Government Printing Office, 1950. p. 232.

VINCENT BECK

Vincent Beck's story serves as an example of a Mennonite's experiences in a Selective Service operated camp. Beck was never at Germfask, but he had been in Mancos and La Pine so he knew most of the men sent to Germfask. In a personal letter to the author, he described his experiences.

June 23, 1980

Dear Mrs. Kopecky:

Being a conscientious objector during the war in CPS Camps was an experience difficult to endure, but later, pleasant to remember. We felt unwelcome everywhere but among camp friends or at home. The government seemed to want us hid away from the public eye. We were not fenced in, there were no armed guards, but there was an invisible fence present, for we knew that if we left unauthorized, or refused to work, we would go to jail.

My thirty-six months of "involuntary servitude" in CPS were very different than most Mennonite men because I spent about sixteen months in Selective Service administered camps at Mancos, Colorado and La Pine, Oregon. I assume I knew most of the men at Germfask, Michigan. The Germfask camp was started by men being transferred from Mancos and La Pine.

I was drafted in the spring of 1943 and found myself in the Grottoes, Virginia CPS camp. The men here were congenial and cooperative Mennonites. After two months, the bulletin board announced that men were needed at the North Fork, California CPS camp. I was one of several who volunteered to go. On the way, our train stopped in Marietta, Ohio.

When our train left Marietta, there were enough men to fill an entire coach car. We were pretty well kept apart from the rest of the passengers. Most of the young men on the train were in military uniform, so we were very noticeable, being young, healthy, and in civilian clothes. When we reached a California station, it was necessary to transfer trains. The CPS men stayed together, and as we left for this second train, a soldier was suddenly in front of me. He asked, "Why are you fellows in civilian clothes?"

I answered, "We all refused to go into the army and the government is sending us to a former Civilian Conservation Camp where we will fight forest fires."

He looked very interested, then shocked, then said, "Why the hell didn't I think of that?"

I opted to go to the first government operated camp opened by Selective Service in July, 1943. It was a former Mennonite camp. I arrived by train with perhaps thirty other men. The camp was about four miles above Mancos. The project was under the direction of the Bureau of Reclamation. We were building an earthen dam on the Mancos River. We were also on alert for forest fire fighting. There was all kinds of earth-moving equipment—trucks, bulldozers, cranes, and hand shovels. There were many test holes in the earth, dug out by hand with a hand winch, rope, bucket, and hand pick and shovel. These holes were about six feet across and thirty feet deep. Purpose was supposedly to determine soil type etc. at certain depths so [an] earthen dam could be properly constructed. The conscientious objectors weren't sure but felt these holes were dug just to make work for the men.

The conscientious objectors in the government administered camps were men predominantly not affiliated with the three peace churches. There were 4,996 of these men scattered throughout the CPS program. Many of these men were activists and protesters, unlike the average Mennonite. This made a noticeable difference between the Selective Service run camps and the Mennonite administered camps. Men in the Selective Service camps were less cooperative, didn't work as conscientiously, and the administration was less sympathetic, less likely to recognize a sick camper, and it was more difficult to get a discharge for being sick. The CO campers at Mancos were a diverse group, and Mennonites were outnumbered considerably, with probably not more than six Mennonites in camp at one time. Many of the men in this camp were well-educated, had a gentle nature, and most had a good sense of humor. Some may have been uncooperative, stubborn, and outspoken. Some were political objectors. Some objected on humane grounds. Others were religious objectors, and some were "war resistors." Some felt CPS camps were (U.S. style) concentration camps where slave labor and involuntary servitude was unconstitutionally sanctioned by the Federal Government.

When an inductee went for his initial physical examination, "conscientious objector" was stamped on his documents. Many unsympathetic doctors declared a CO physically fit regardless of his health. (Some) COs were drafted into CPS who would have been rejected by the armed forces (4F-medical discharge).

One injustice in CPS was when a camper became ill. If you were sick, you asked for a SQ (sick quarters) so you would not have to work that day. Some men would say they were sick but could not get a SQ. They would then work while ill or refuse to work and be charged with RTW (refusal to work). If a camper got so many RTWs, he would end up in prison. At La Pine and Mancos, I learned how SQ requests could be pushed to the limit.

When Mancos reached maximum capacity, men were transferred to a new government camp in La Pine, Oregon, also a former Mennonite camp. As the Mancos men moved in, the Mennonites moved out.

We called it "Camp Wickiup." Wickiup Reservoir is the second largest reservoir in the United States. It was created by damming the Deschutes River, a project completed about 1949.

We were housed in a former CCC camp about twenty miles into the forest from La Pine, a remote cross-road community with only a post office. Bend, Oregon, was another thirty miles down the road.

The camp was on the Deschutes River, a fast-moving clear stream full of trout. Former President Hoover had a cabin along this stream. The project was to clear and remove the trees and vegetation from the area where the water would be impounded after the dam was built. The dam and water impounded was for an irrigation project. The campsite, then, is now inundated.

In Camp Wickiup was a group of men, not Mennonites, who were ready and willing to go to prison, men who were antiwar, anti-conscription, and anti-slavery, and didn't hesitate to let the government men know. These men wrote songs, insulting but cleverly worded. They gave copies to the men in camp. At the first meal in the dining room, we were advised that the songs would be sung. The dining room was segregated, with Mennonite campers seated together, the "Mancos Group" seated together, and the camp administrators together at the head table. The government men and the Mennonite campers were aghast when the "Mancos Group" boldly sang this song.

(In camp, everything was signaled with a bell. When it was time to eat, the bell would ring; when it was time to go to work, a bell would ring, etc. Olsen was the camp administrator.)

"OLD MAN OLSEN HAD A CAMP"

To tune of "Old McDonald Had a Farm"
Old man Olsen had a camp,
E-I-E-I-O.
And in this camp were Menn-O-nites.
E-I-E-I-O
With a yes, yes, here, a yes, yes, there,
Here a yes, there a yes,
Everywhere a yes, yes.

Old man Olsen had a camp,
E-I-E-I-O.

And in this camp there was a bell,
E-I-E-I-O.
With a ding, ding here, a dong, dong, there,
Here a ding, there a dong, everywhere a ding, dong.

Old man Olsen had a camp,
E-I-E-I-O.
And in this camp there were Manco-sites,
E-I-E-I-O.
With a no, no, here,
A no, no, there,
Here a no, there a no,
Everywhere a "HELL, no!"
Old man Olsen had a camp,
E-I-E-I-O.

This was the only camp I was in that had indoor recreation facilities—a gymnasium. In our spare time, we wrote letters, played
checkers or chess, or listened to crystal radio. One fellow trapped
coyotes. Some of the fellows cut firewood to sell. There were no
chainsaws then. The natives burned firewood in two to four feet
lengths. There were usually enough country musicians in camp
to have a band on weekends. There were hikes and backpacking.
Occasionally, some would ride into Bend, Oregon, in the rear of
the crew truck to go to church. Very few of the natives would ever
visit the camp, and the campers felt unwelcome most places they
went. I don't recall any community near a CPS camp that made
any effort to know what was going on.

One camper was an excellent chess player. He could play ten
different people at the same time while blindfolded and would usually win all the games. Each time his opponent moved, the move
was told to this young man. He remembered each board and the
moves. Girls were nonexistent in camp life unless friends or relatives came to visit or unless the camper went home on furlough.

The campers as I knew them had minds of their own. I don't
recall one fight between campers, or any physical abuse between
campers and the administration. There was on occasion verbal
abuse between campers and administration. The campers did not
all believe in non-resistance. Some believed in "non-violence,"

some in "non-cooperation." Some perhaps believed in self-defense but not organized warfare or conscription.

I remember an incident that happened here. Danny Dingman was a small young man and very uncooperative with the work program. He was antiwar, anti-conscription, and he didn't want to cooperate with the work project because he said it was involuntary servitude. The first day at our worksite, Danny stayed in the truck until Tom, the boss, told him to get out. He reluctantly got out and just stood there. Tom ordered, "Take your axe and get busy!"

Dan said, "I don't know what to do. I never had an axe before."

Tom, cursing, took Danny over to a tree and said, "The sawyers can't get to the tree to saw it down with those branches growing so close to the ground. Take the axe and cut those branches off."

Danny was enjoying the situation. Tom showed Dan how to cut a branch off and Danny got to work. Tom walked away mumbling. Some time later, Tom came back, and looking around, couldn't find Danny.

Danny was about twenty feet off the ground, way up in the tree, with all the branches cut off below him.

Tom said, "What are you doing up there?"

Danny answered, "I can't get down! I don't know how to get down."

More mumbling.

Danny's philosophy was, "If I am going to be treated like a slave, I will act like one."

Another incident involved Johnny Calef. You must remember that this was an all-male camp. No women. Johnny was sunbathing between the dormitory buildings naked. A government man turned him in to the Bend, Oregon, police.

JOHNNY BOY

Tune: "Billy Boy"
Oh, where have you gone, Johnny boy, Johnny boy?
Oh, where have you gone, Johnny Calef?
Some filthy minded prude,

Said he saw you in the nude,
You're a young thing and
Shouldn't leave your mother.

Do you want to go to jail, Johnny boy, Johnny boy?
Do you want to go to jail, Johnny Calef?
Except for SQ [sick quarters]
It will seem the same to you,
You have gone from one prison
To another.

Are you sorry to be gone, Johnny boy, Johnny boy?
Are you sorry to be gone, Johnny Calef?
You really shouldn't care.
The administration won't be there,
That is something that should
Make you happy, BROTHER.

WHO'S GOING NEXT?

'Twas at a camp named Wickiup
And all the lads were there
A-raising holy blazes
In the middle of Murch's [camp manager] hair,

Refrain

**Singing who's going next, lads,
Who's going to jail?
You'd better be a-ready
With your pockets full of bail.**

And Uncle Elmer [work superintendent] came along
A-driving thru the fog
And who should be a-sittin' there
Behind him but his dog.

Refrain

And Pollard [bookkeeper] was a-sittin' there
A-messin' up the books
And when he couldn't balance 'em
He blamed it on the cooks.

Refrain

And Herby Murch was also there
And very pleased to see
Four-and-twenty COs
A-hanging from a tree.

Refrain

One day a list of the bad boys, the vocal and non-cooperative men picked by the Government Camp Administration, was posted. They were to be transferred to a camp in Germfask, Michigan, so a new song was posted.

MICHIGAN

To the tune of "Song of Notre Dame"

M-I-C-H-I-G-A-N
We all know that this will be the end,
One way passage to Germfask,
The cold storage spot for the bad boy class.

We don't believe that slavery is right.
We fight it in our own way, with might.
So off to Michigan are we,
And onward to liberty.

OUR OLD AND DUSTY LOAM

Oh the bad boys gone
From the forests of La Pine,
They've left for a camp in Michigan
The director thinks all the brains have gone with them,
But we'll carry on the work the "Slobs" began.

So weep no more for Mancos;
The brains are not all gone
We will sing this song to our friends so far away
And the fight which they began
Carry on!

From La Pine, Oregon, I went to Lyons, New Jersey, where I was one of perhaps 100 or more CPS who men worked in a Brethren Church Service unit at a veterans' mental hospital as an attendant (thirteen months). General Omar Bradley was in charge of the hospital. This was more interesting since we were back to civilization and we received $15 a month. After twelve months at the hospital, the war ended. People were starving in Poland, Germany, etc. so the United States Government organized the United Nations Relief and Rehabilitation Administration to bring food and relief supplies to them. I left New Jersey for Newport, Virginia, where a group of CPS men boarded the *Plymouth Victory* ship loaded with 900 horses (to be used as farm horses). The men cared for these horses while sailing across the Atlantic to Gdynia, Poland. We were told most of them were eaten to prevent starvation.

Upon return of the empty ship to Norfolk, Virginia, I received my discharge from CPS and hitch-hiked home to Pittsville, Ohio.

Sincerely,   Vincent Beck

VINCENT BECK COLLECTION

The following four pictures were taken at Camp Wickiup. Mr. Beck identified the men.

Left: Tiny, camp cook. Second man unknown.

The men in this photograph were transferred to Germfask.
Front row left: Unknown, Frank Hatfield, George Baird
Back row left: Dave Miller, Nick Migliorino, John (Banjo) Marsh, Al
Partridge, John Neubrand, "Ike" Bjorn Eikrem, Jack Smock.

Bottom left: unknown, George Baird, unknown, Bjorn Eikrem (Ike), Jack Smock
Top row left: Al Partridge, unknown, Johnny Calef

The conscientious objectors were transferred to this vacated CCC Camp located on the outskirts of town.

NORMAN NELSON

1989 Interview at Nelson Home in Seney, Michigan

Mr. Nelson was the camp director and only one of three government paid officials who "stuck it out" at Camp Germfask. He lived in Seney all his life, with the exception of time spent in the service before World War II.

It's not a subject I like to talk about, period. I've never talked about it with anyone except my wife, not even my close friends. I was summoned to Washington several times to testify. I don't want to get into specifics. It was a job; it was just a job I got paid to do. That's all there is to it. Several of the campers tried to draw me into conversation at work, and several asked if they could visit me at my home to explain their position. I refused to talk with them and refused to let them into my house. One of them sent me a letter. I refused to acknowledge it.

WORK SUPERINTENDENT C.S. JOHNSON'S

SUMMARY OF CPS135

Highlights of the Year
Seney National Wildlife Refuge, Germfask, Michigan
1944-1945

Following is Johnson's required summary to the National Park Service explaining the amount of work completed during 1944-1945 by the conscientious objectors assigned to do work at the Seney National Wildlife Refuge.

These pages are furnished by request, but reluctantly. We would prefer to forget the whole thing.

Up to May 12, 1944, events pursued the even tenor of their way at this station, even up to the bright noon of that day when a few employees of the Fish and Wildlife Service and a bunch of strangers classified as conscientious objectors sat down to a fine dinner of roast pork, mashed potatoes and rich brown gravy, combination salad, tender green peas, hot buns, a selection of two kinds of pie, and coffee. The proud cook beamed through the spotless glitter of the kitchen as he watched his provender being stowed away. Administrative personnel, exuding good humor and religious belief, covertly sized up their new charges and made plans for using Whoozis and Henry Whatcanacallit for this and that. Up to 12:35 p.m. of May 12, 1944, official life on the Seney Refuge was normal, if not fine. Most everybody had by then licked up the last delicious morsel of pie, and convinced himself that Archie was one hell of a swell cook. It was about time for the speech of welcome.

At 12:35:52, the froth of sprightly, highly educated chit-chat was rudely silenced by the sound of clanking chains and a shatteringly voice declaiming, "This is slavery!" It was Bishop, a veteran of five camps, putting on his act, the main features of which were a ball and chain and a string of "quotations." Bishop, with the traditional beard of the prophets and other stage effects consisting of a Bible, an ascetic face, and a fanatical gleam in his eye.

In our innocence, we immediately concluded that Bishop was a screwball and, as such, eligible to be in the sanitarium some twenty-six miles away. Arrangements were made that very day to put the gentleman in his proper environment, but the idea was abandoned upon instructions from Washington. We learned later that Bishop was just a fair sample of the CO group and his act, and his objective in using it, was one of many which were characteristic of the type of objectors selected for the Germfask camp. Bishop was one of the twenty or thirty objectors who were later sent to Federal prison. Even there he carried on his crusade for something or other, starving himself for eighty-six days, obtaining bonded release for an appeal, jilting bondsmen, and finally ending up in prison under a four-year sentence. We no longer hear about Bishop, but his spirit must have infested the camp, for it got no better during his absence, and his disciples kept the place in a constant ferment up to the day when the camp made the headlines.

Up to that inevitable climax, every day at camp was a chapter in itself, with the objectors trying to break up the camp by every means available, including the stealing of mess equipment, such as dishes, stove doors, and lids; theft and destruction of food; sabotage of the water supply system and the sewage system; hiding or stealing of working equipment; even putting broken glass in the garbage to the irritation of the poor pigs which might well have fattened on this byproduct for the American war effort. The objective of the administration in this contest was to hold on until new regulations could be written to cure the situation. The objectors' purpose was to show that the set-up would not work and the only solution was to crash through with discharges for all the dissenters in the camp.

The deadlocked situation existed up to the last few days of the camp's existence, when a few men were sent away for reclassification to the armed services, or failing to do so (and we don't know if any really were inducted), were sent to prison. During the thirteen months of the camp's duration, personnel changes were many, for the various positions were hardly to be desired. Five cooks and five camp managers, in particular, were hired during that period. The camp director, the project superintendent, two foremen, the camp clerk, and the mechanic stuck it through. Four camp doctors had a go at the "sick list," and special medical boards also had their fingers on the pulse of the camp. Specialists, FBI agents, state police, U.S. Department of Justice officials, parole officers representing the Federal prisons, writers of all kinds, representatives of antiwar groups, American Legion delegations, several U.S. congressmen, inspectors of various Federal agencies came—and went.

It can be truthfully said that the main activity of this camp was refusal to work. Those who were inclined to do so contributed the following to the work program here:

road graveling	4.5	miles
new fence, goose pen	2.0	miles
fence repair:		
boundary posts and wire	13	miles
fire fighting	300	acres
roadside cleanup	2	miles
razing buildings	1	sawmill
upland planting	7	acres
clearing	6	acres
erosion control applied	125	tons of hay

dike repair:

¾ mile of C-2 dike

1 mile of T-2 dike

1/10 mile of A-2 dike

In examining the cloud which has hovered over the place this past year, the silver lining seems to be substantial in the way of cash revenue, and somewhat thin in the amount of productive labor. It is estimated that the value of road gravel, posts, wire, paint, hay, and other miscellaneous supplies approximates $20,000.00. The labor performed by working foremen, the machine shop operator, and the camp clerk (who also handled refuge paperwork), and the labor done on the above-named projects by objectors was worth about $15,000.00. In other words, the net return to this refuge was about $35,000.00. Yet to be realized is the transfer of all camp equipment, the camp itself, and small hand and shop tools.

CHESTER OSBORNE

Personal Documents

I, Chester C. Osborne, was responsible for the behavior of the men and also their spiritual advisor. I also was pastoring a Mennonite Church, The Fernland Congregation, located in the Germfask community. The church, although small in membership, was a significant force in the area.

My participation in the Camp Germfask story has never been widely publicized, and probably even less understood. Jane M. Kopecky of Gulliver, Michigan, recently appealed to me to write my participation in the story. I have decided to furnish her with several letters and papers. I think these give my reason for accepting the assignment, as well as, after understanding the reasons for their [COs] inability to cooperate, my decision after three months to resign as camp manager.

The government men stated that since the Mennonites had been successful in the operation of their [conscientious objectors] camps [elsewhere], they were hoping that having a Mennonite minister in charge of the camp would be the key to success for them at Germfask. It soon became apparent that Selective Service had been less than honest in its plans and expectations for this camp.

…I was uninformed until May 11, the day before the arrival of the first assignees, that this was to be a camp where as administrators, we were to carry notebooks to the intent of gathering information, quotations, etc. with the expressed purpose of building up a case for the FBI to prosecute and imprison some, to send others to insane asylums, that these were "outlaws and saboteurs", quoting Victor Olson.

These men had been "weeded out" of the other government camps... Selective Service really didn't care if the men at Germfask worked, or didn't work. They were to be in a holding pattern.

Out of respect to Mr. Clarence Johnson, the Camp Director, I felt it unwise to resign immediately without at least endeavoring to find the motive that caused these men to be classified as they were. I had understood in coming into the administration of the camp that my unofficial job was to study them and help them to respond, if such were possible, not to try my utmost to send them to prison. This did not coincide with my original understanding.

The adversities of life in general, and of conscription in particular, always does one of two things to us. It either develops us into better people, or else into more degraded personalities.... I came to the conclusion that an undesirable reaction was developing in my own mental being.

These men were judged by the fact that they were not ready and willing manual laborers. The Germfask community did not understand them, and I think the Mennonite Church didn't understand either, and were equally unable to help them. They questioned the integrity of the church's program of "Work of National Importance," as well as the government's methods available to them to get the rest of us to try to understand.

SOME OF MY MEMORIES OF No. 135

The first contingent of men arrived at about 10:00 a.m. Staff helped them unload and assigned them to cots in the barracks. I then went to the dining room to assist the cook. After a dinner bell sounded the call for the men to come, I heard a loud KLUNK at the entry. One man had carried a ball to attract attention, then shuffled his way to a table. After lunch, in talking to him, I found the ball was actually made of wood and not padlocked on at all. This was one of his ways of saying, "I am a slave, a man in bondage to Selective Service."

This was Corbett Bishop, the most notorious of the incorrigible conscientious objectors and an "instant legend in CPS before he went to prison." He was a devoted follower of Gandhi and carried on many fasts, one in Germfask. He was a free spirit who offered sardonic commentary and pacifist readings in the dining hall during mealtime, usually to the delight and applause of his fellow campers and to the annoyance of the camp administrative personnel. One day, to everyone's surprise, he read a lengthy statement blatantly extolling military glory and nationalism. When he sat down, he was applauded, but only by those at the camp administration table. He then rose again to announce, to the uproarious delight of the conscientious objectors, that the passage he had read was taken from Adolf Hitler's *Mein Kampf.*

As an illustration of the Mahatma Gandhi non-violent type of techniques they used, Mr. Saunders, the work foreman out on the field projects, took a group to saw up some fallen trees. They waited for him to direct each move as, "Bring the cross-cut saw. Two of you take the handles. Now pull it. No, only one pull. O.K., now quit pulling, and the other man pull, you push. You quit pulling, now start pushing, let the first man pull."

Mr. Saunders was a very kind and jovial man, yet eventually even he could no longer out-strategize them in this type of exaggerated literal over-obedience. In the final weeks, no pretense of work was maintained.

The plan was that inductees should help in the kitchen, dining, and housekeeping details. Some liked the kitchen broken shift as it gave them free time to themselves. Others declined to assume any responsibility even in supplying their own needs. Their reasoning was, "Selective Service brought me here; you can take care of me."

The original chef was a very well-trained and competent man. I used Army manuals to set up menus and order supplies for the kitchen, yet some men complained quite frequently. Eventually, only a few men cooperated to help in the kitchen and dining details. The tension became subtle until the cook, whom I felt was doing an excellent job, began to fear the men, became *a*pprehensive, and then suddenly resigned. He was replaced by another man.

I was only in charge for three months, but as I remember, later on a few of the men did the food preparation themselves. Nighttime break-ins into the kitchen and food stocks became more frequent. The stocks were moved into the building the staff used as headquarters. Food was issued for each meal, and the men could prepare it as they pleased. In the final weeks, the kitchen dining building burned. No one seemed to know the cause.

The first few days of the existence of the camp, two men appeared one evening at the village tavern to purchase a few drinks. Soon the community people knew about the incident and concluded, "These men are not real conscientious objectors or they wouldn't drink!" Finally, the village was made off-limits to the men.

I found a package marked "Storm Flag." Thinking it was a weather flag to be used in a marine harbor, I remarked, "I don't see how we will have any use for that." An elderly man allowed to stay in the camp as a watchman and caretaker overheard me saying that. The community soon was saying that I would not use the American Flag in the camp. Examining the package more closely, I found it really was an official U.S. flag, made rugged enough to withstand stormy weather. This statement of mine didn't help the CO image [or the Mennonite image] in the community.

As I remember, one of the government staff men would drive a truck periodically to Newberry or Manistique. Usually only a few men would go for the outing or change. One Sunday afternoon, six or eight men rode the truck to Newberry. I don't remember the details that precipitated the action, but a small and angry crowd gathered to drive the men out of their city. The men wanted to cooperate, but one member was missing. After cruising for a while, he appeared, and they escaped. Some of them stated to me that they really feared for their lives.

One young man, who was a model assignee, desired to bring his wife and small daughter to be near him. He could arrange that she should live with one of the prominent families in the town, working as a maid and cook for herself and the daughter's room and board plus a very small salary. This was approved and for some weeks seemed to be going quite well. We lived about two and one-half miles out into the rural area. One evening when I was off-duty, the young husband appeared at our door to inform me that he had a problem. The community feeling was so adverse that the family had requested his wife to leave. He wanted to get her out of the town that night. Eva, my wife, and I counseled for a few minutes and decided that we should take the young wife and daughter into our home. They stayed for some weeks, then returned to Ohio to live with one of their parents.

Some of the men were chronically ill and probably should never have been drafted originally. They could report for sick call each morning, or I visited them on their cots. We had no nurse, only a first aid station, and no one qualified to daily and properly prescribe for them. Area doctors occasionally visited, but their offices were thirty miles away. Selective Service called some of these men "malingerers" and maybe they were, but I wasn't competent to so label them. If I remember correctly, a few men who finally walked out and subsequently were arrested, as well as a few who asked for transfer into the Army, were given proper physical examinations and declared 4F, or physically unfit. One must wonder, "Why did it take so many years?"

I think that today by present military standards most all those Camp Germfask men would be classified, "Mentally unfit for military duty," and sent home. Yet I remember that in the fever of the war-time regimentation, Selective Service felt they had to remove the conscientious objectors away from their own communities.

Camp Germfask was a disappointment to the Seney National Wildlife Refuge, in the small amount of productive work obtained. In the approximate year of the camp's existence, there was very little open exchange or endeavor by the community people to listen or understand the men. I think that my wife and I were probably the only persons of the Mennonite Church there who tried to keep open an avenue of receptive helpfulness. The men of Camp Germfask were by and large unwanted men. Not ministered to by their own denominations, and removing themselves from the church administered camps, they had only their own spiritual strengths to endure the experience. With some that was not sufficient, while others came out helped and more matured.

CHESTER OSBORNE: BY FLORENCE WEAVER

Letter

Florence Weaver was Chester Osborne's sister-in-law. She stayed with the Osbornes for several weeks during the summer of 1944. Following are excerpts from a letter she sent the author on February 17, 1980.

Dear Jane,

…Many of the men had been college students, at least for a short time.

Government authorities asked Chester to have oversight of the camp. He agreed to do so after much consideration. He soon decided that was a mistake because of the types of and kinds of men they were. He stayed with the job for a short time and resigned.

The men were very unruly and hard to manage. They had good supplies of food, etc. Finally refrigerators and supplies had to be locked at night.

They would tear around disgracefully at night as far as Newberry, or maybe further. It seems their response was to get even with the government authorities for keeping them there instead of letting them be as free citizens. It probably was draft authorities controlling them.

Chester made an attempt to have services with them at times but with little success. They were just not spiritually minded. They claimed conscientious objection without a background for it.

The community did not accept the men nor the camp. The church work was greatly affected by them. The people of the area concluded the church was responsible for putting the camp there, and some refused to attend church any more or to send children to Bible school.

Chester tried to explain to the people the difference in the belief of the Mennonite Church and a government-controlled camp like this. The church's beliefs were based on Christ's teaching of love and peace and the sacredness of human life. Of course, people had their minds set and would not accept an explanation. Some of the older residents of Germfask still talk about this experience when they have the opportunity. The younger folks do not know about it, only as they have heard from older ones.

Florence

BRUCE HANDRICH

1980 Personal Interview

Bruce Handrich arrived in Germfask in 1947 to become the Mennonite Pastor. He and his wife Savilla were despised by community members because they knew Bruce had been in Civilian Public Service, and they associated him with Osborne and Camp Germfask. When Bruce or Savilla walked down the street, people would move to the other side to avoid them. Savilla said the hardest thing she ever did was send her two young children to school. Bruce took a stand. He asked the local American Legion if he could speak at one of its meetings. He told them about his beliefs and his conscientious objector experience, after which, residents began to accept him. Eventually, he became one of their most respected and liked citizens.

"Some people still associate me with the Germfask camp and believe that I was there. I was not in the Germfask camp. The smoke jumpers came into existence during this time with most of the original jumpers being conscientious objectors. I was in a smoke jumpers unit out west. News about Germfask spread to all the CPS camps. We were very much aware of what was happening.

"The men (COs) worked on farm programs, in mental hospitals, or irrigation or reclamation projects. Some men volunteered as human guinea pigs in medical experiments. The government did not want CPS to interfere with the war effort, so they took a great deal of care to make sure these programs would not be publicized. They did not want it to escalate beyond what it was. They did, however, encourage publicity of the Germfask camp because it stirred up public resentment. That publicity kept the focus off the humanitarian projects being done in other CPS camps.

"Some of these men were older men. They had given up good-paying salaries for their convictions. The government offered them alternative jobs within the government, but they refused them. They could have led a sheltered life. These men were intelligent, probably some of the smartest men in the country. A lawyer I met in La Pine, Oregon, who was eventually sent to Germfask, was probably the most intelligent person I have ever conversed with.

"Our local church was drawn into this emotionally charged situation. The community assumed the church had invited these men to Germfask.

"A neighbor threatened to burn down the church. Rumors circulated that Mr. Osborne was to be tarred and feathered. There were also rumors of an attempted lynching. Many threats were made; threats that, maybe, if the opportunity and the situation were right, might have happened. Tension was high.

"Osborne knew the only way the church would survive is if he left the area."

DR. ROBERT CORDELL

May 1980 phone interview

"I was in that camp. We called Germfask the Siberian Concentration Camp. The men there were sophisticated in their beliefs; they had a lot of education and most were college men. We had many intellectual-type bull sessions. Many of the men brought their own libraries with professional-type literature. I was going to do my Ph.D. thesis on the fossils I had collected in the Germfask area. I just disposed of them a short while ago."

When I told Dr. Cordell of my early memories and the man with the funny cap, he explained that he always wore his cap with the bill turned to the side. He had been the man holding the gunnysack, the man collecting rocks in our barnyard.

In 1997, I received a phone call from Dr. Cordell's son. He wanted to inform me that his father had passed away and the family was curious about a copy of a letter they found in his desk. It was addressed to me and was on top of his papers, in a position easy to find. I told him I had received the letter in 1980. (It was the letter to follow.)

The letter surprised Dr. Cordell's son because he didn't know his father had been a conscientious objector. He went on to say, "He was a private man. He didn't force his opinions on us and he encouraged us to think for ourselves. He was a good listener who didn't talk much about himself."

Dr. Cordell earned a PhD in geology from the University of Missouri in 1949. He was associated with Sun Oil Company, and a highly respected geologist, publishing numerous scientific reports in his area of expertise. He served several terms as president of the Geological Society of America. He was a founding member and president of the Richardson [Texas] Symphony Orchestra and an original member of the Church of the Transfiguration (Episcopal) in Dallas, signing the articles of incorporation. (Dr. Cordell's scientific reports can be found online.)

ROBERT CORDELL LETTER OF JUNE 20, 1980

Dear Mrs. Kopecky,

Please excuse my delayed reply—I have been quite busy lately with my geological report business, and also in helping put on a recent annual convention for petroleum geologists in Denver.

Needless to say, I was quite surprised by your phone call about Germfask, after so many intervening years. Thanks very much for copies of the newspaper clippings—they brought back many memories of the people and the experience at the camp.

I have included small "thumb-nail" sketches of the men whose pictures or quotes appeared in the Escanaba paper; and also of thirty or so other "campers" at Germfask. Hopefully, this will provide some insight into the wide variety of men who were stationed there. The common denominator was strong conscientious objection to war; but otherwise, there were almost as many types as people.

Again, thanks for getting in touch with me, and the best of good fortune in the future.

Sincerely, Robert J. Cordell

THUMBNAIL SKETCHES OF GERMFASK CAMPERS
By Robert Cordell

Camp Germfask was a government CPS camp operated and financed by Selective Service. It was populated mostly by men who had not adjusted well in the church-sponsored CPS camps or projects that were scattered around the country.

The nature and reason for the lack of adjustment were almost as varied as the number of individuals represented. For some, it was a matter of conscience against conscription. These men would work at a slower pace than acceptable, or they would become extreme literalists and do only precisely what they were told to do, to the letter. This resulted in such things as pounding numerous staples around fence wire to a single post when one or two would do. A few would go on hunger strikes as a demonstration against conscription. A small percentage opted to go to prison from the church camps, as a more drastic form of witnessing. They simply walked out of camp, knowing they would be picked up and sent to prison.

At Camp Wellston, Michigan (near Manistee), a Church of the Brethren camp, I did not keep a militarily tidy bunk, and I hung my own poetry on the wall above it. Even though a literary critic who visited the camp praised my efforts and advised me to pursue a writing career, my bunk was not exactly what either Selective Service or the Church of the Brethren sponsors had in mind for sleeping quarters. Thus I was ticketed for a transfer to Germfask.

Other inmates of the church camps simply were not "cut out" for work in the forest. The labor projects management of most of the camps was conducted by the United States Bureau of Forestry because those camps were located in national forests as a means of isolating the conscientious objectors from the public. Naturally, the Bureau of Forestry wanted work projects for the conscientious objectors that would contribute to their programs. So we sawed down and chopped up second-growth deciduous trees in areas better fitted for pine forests. Thus, lumbering work was done in the fall and winter; then in the spring and summer, we planted small pine trees. We always were on twenty-four-hour call in case of forest fires. I did not mind the physical work because I found it therapeutic to some extent, and I was strong enough physically to handle it without any problem, having been raised on a farm. I actually saw the work as a contribution, and I did a better than average job. But as noted above, many of the "campers" adjusted poorly to the work because they had no background for it and were not physically equipped. A fair percentage of these people wound up on an involuntary transfer list, one of the destinations being Germfask. About the only alternative to forestry in the church-sponsored projects was work in mental hospitals. A fair percentage of the men applied for and received transfers to mental hospitals to help take care of the patients, as better witness to their beliefs. Some were successful, but others found this work extremely difficult and frustrating, mainly because the hospitals' managements often were bureaucratic organizations without much positive concern for the poor unfortunate confines.

Still other conscientious objectors adjusted poorly in the church camps because of a strong conviction that they could be doing something much more worthwhile for the pacifist cause or for the world at large than the cutting down and planting of trees, or the waiting for forest fires that very seldom, if ever, materialized. This group included some of the most highly intellectual people in the camps. Many of these men were active in pacifist group gatherings, discussions, and pacifist literature study. Such activities were permitted as long as the individual put in a hard day every work day in the woods. But if he did not, for whatever reason, he became a likely candidate for Germfask.

A minor percentage of the men could not cope mentally with the combination of being isolated, working for essentially no pay at tasks they disliked, having no privacy, and seeing no end to camp internment. Some of these men developed mildly neurotic behavior or became seriously depressed. Part were given 4-F classifications and were dismissed from the service: part were sent to Germfask or other destinations. There seemed to be little logic to the decisions that were made in these cases, except that if the camp director or Selective Service took a personal dislike to the man, he stood a good chance of being shipped to the Germfask camp, or some other less livable camp, apparently as a punitive measure.

A few men in the church camps were non-conformists in the strict sense of the word, and as a mode of everyday living. A refusal to work was sometimes the chief expression of their beliefs. A portion of this small group was sent to Germfask.

The above discussion hopefully gives some idea of the varied backgrounds of the men who were assigned to the Germfask camp. While I was there, I doubt whether the camp roster stood at more than fifty. Roughly two-thirds were highly intelligent, college-educated intellectual types, most of whom led exemplary lives and were seriously attempting to do something they thought would improve society. A small proportion were active members of minor political parties such as the Socialists or Social-Laborites, but there were no communists. The other one-third were less educated, their experience consisting of farming, industrial labor, or a skilled trade. This contingent included several Jehovah's Witnesses, a few who belonged to fundamentalist religious groups, a minor sprinkling of men who were difficult to classify, and probably three or four 18-20 year-olds who did not constitute a cohesive group.

My arrival at Germfask coincided with the official opening of the camp to conscientious objectors. The first week we had meat and potatoes but no other food because nothing else had arrived yet. In the months that followed, there was no attempt by the camp management to organize an official overall work project of any kind. A few men would be asked to go somewhere to mend a fence or cut weeds beside a road, or something else—with only a vague idea, if any, of how, or by whom, these assignments had been created or determined. Clearly the attitude of the camp management was that it would try to get some effort out of the assignees, but it was difficult to escape the conclusion that most of the assignments were "made-work" to keep the men physically busy. There was very little if any camp planning or organization. Nearly all of us were convinced that the primary purpose was one of incarceration and isolation. The chief duty of the management obviously was to "keep the lid on," whether or not any work worthy of the name was done.

In this environment, the reactions of the men took predictable turns. All of the better-educated did a great deal of reading. Some of them spent considerable time conducting correspondence by letter, mostly on matters related to pacifism and conscription. Others, including myself, decided to make the best of the situation by continuing the professional careers, in whatever guise possible, that we had begun prior to being drafted. Among this latter group were three lawyers, one of whom advised assignees of their legal positions vis-à-vis Selective Service in various contingencies that might emerge. Some of the more ingenious assignees established the so-called Tobacco Road as an attempt to lighten the confinement. Their attitude was that "Stone walls do not a prison make," necessarily. Part of this group were writers and artists. Most of the lesser-educated assignees became depressed and despondent. To them, the place was like a prison, and unfortunately, they did not have the imagination or background to make it anything else.

(Toujours gai is French for "always cheerful." Tobacco Road was a 1932 novel by Erskine Caldwell about the living conditions of poor Georgia sharecroppers. Their sometimes humorous antics depict the consequences of poverty, racism, and low moral standards. *Life Magazine* included it as one of the 100 outstanding books between 1924-1944, and it became a Broadway play that ran for eight years.)

GERMFASK "CAMPERS" PUBLICIZED IN *ESCANABA DAILY PRESS*

Captions verbatim from the newspaper, Tuesday, February 6, 1945

Geologist-R. J. Cordell, of Emden, IL, a graduate of the University of Missouri, is a geologist who devotes much of his time to the study of native stones at Germfask.

Some Privacy *– Gerald Dingman is shown here in his private boudoir along "Tobacco Road." It is complete with draw curtains and all.* [This newspaper caption is incorrect. Dan Dingman is pictured here as evidenced by his notorious cap.]

TOUJOURS GAI – *First to strike your eyes upon entering "Tobacco Road," the barracks of the individualists. There is also a pot of brew on hand. In this picture are Gerald Dingman and Daniel Dingman, of Palmer, Massachusetts, and Paul Browder, of Denison, Texas.* [Daniel is left and wearing his cap; Gerald is center.]

ARTIST – *Batsell Moore, of Waco, Texas is the camp artist and is shown with some of his paintings, which include portraits and landscape scenes.*

PIN UP-ROW – *"Tobacco Road" claims to have the best collection of pin-ups of any CO camp in the country. Only a few of the full assortment are shown here in this photo, which features Paul Browder and his mandolin.*

ACCORDIONIST – *The CPS service camp at Germfask has several musicians, among them Paul Chowder, of Marion, Ohio. Paul is shown here in one of his musical moments.*

CARPENTER – *Leonard Lewis, of Webster Grove, Missouri, is a carpenter, at least by avocation. He is pictured here with a tackle box that he made from scrap lumber. He also had a tool chest expertly made in his spare time.*

CAMP BARRACKS – *This is one of the conventional barracks at the CPS camp at Germfask. Cots and equipment conform generally to regulation. Officials say that the occupants of this barracks are among the most cooperative assignees to the camp.*

CAMP OFFICIALS – *The executive staff is headed by Norman V. Nelson, camp director, left, and Earl R. Walz, camp manager, who are shown here in their office.*

WOOD CUTTER – *Sol Gadol, New York, hauls fuel wood into one of the buildings at the camp. Wood cutting is one of the important jobs at the camp.*

STUDENT – *John Chester, of Brooklyn, New York, is a student of religion and is studying the Bible is this picture, while his dog looks on.*

(Cordell Letter continues below)

Gerald Dingman – A very level-headed older man (probably thirty or so) who enjoyed informal surroundings (like "Tobacco Road") took a fatherly interest in some of the younger men and was always available to give advice or counsel. Highly intelligent and well-read. The family owned some kind of business in Palmer, Massachusetts.

Daniel Dingman – Younger brother of Gerald, he was both pleasant and enthusiastic. His dedication was demonstrated by the fact that, after much thought and contemplation, he decided to walk out of camp to face arrest and imprisonment.

Paul Browder – A young carefree type from Texas. Liked country music and played a good mandolin.

Batsell Moore – An excellent artist who had received some praise from art critics. Very strong-minded and dedicated in his opposition to conscription.

Sol Gadol – Quiet, unassuming, and methodical, he had been a tin-smith, but not sure whether this was his vocation or avocation.

Leonard Lewis – No doubt he already has sent some information on himself. Was very courageous and strong-minded in his opposition to conscription.

Paul Crowder – Black, one of the older assignees, with a lot of life experience—a practical philosopher. He seemed at home in any surroundings. A fine musician, excellent on the accordion.

John Chester – Italian ancestry; he was quite young and had an unusually personalized religion. In addition to his religious studies, he was one of the most complete altruists I have ever known. Also had an infectious sense of humor. When the camp doctor, who also was of Italian lineage, made his occasional visits, John delighted in engaging him in conversation—in Italian.

George Baird – Had been in the advertising business in New York City. An older man, probably in his late thirties at the time, he had been a track star as a student at the University of Iowa, and had been a member of a winning relay team in the Olympics. He was a Theosophist; the founder of this sect was a Russian woman. Very dedicated.

OTHER GERMFASK "CAMPERS"

[Note below that people are numbered rather than named. Dr. Cordell did not provide names out of respect for these individuals' privacy because they were not listed in the newspapers.]

No. 1 – A Ph.D. in chemistry; also a good laborer and mechanic. Had good research position with DuPont prior to war; resigned it when his conscience no longer would allow him to participate in DuPont's chemical industry for war. He decided to walk out of the Germfask camp as a further gesture of conscience, knowing he would be picked up and imprisoned.

No. 2 – A faculty member at an eastern college before being drafted; a brilliant and humorous person who was highly regarded by his fellows.

No. 3 – Had been a graduate student in biology at a mid-western university. Was interested in all the wildlife around the camp area.

No. 4 – A lawyer from the east, of Jewish background, who spent a great deal of time counseling the camp members about the legal aspects of the Selective Service law. Spent hours with some of the relatively uneducated men. Very sincere in everything he did.

No. 5 – A lawyer from Pennsylvania who was trying to stay abreast of his specialty—laws having to do with inheritance. Excellent conversationalist, witty.

No. 6 – A lawyer who had graduated from Harvard. Took a great interest in getting to know the various men in the camp. Dated a local girl in the Germfask area when he could get leave— apparently without serious repercussions.

No. 7 – A gifted writer from California, who planned sometime to write "the great American novel." Also a good poet and brilliant conversationalist. I have seen reference to him a couple of times since in literary magazines as an established author, who, last I heard, lived in Nevada.

No. 8. – An artist who was thoroughly interested in the pacifist movement. He read voraciously and was a highly cultured individual. Also had good writing ability.

No. 9 – An excellent organizer and activist in the pacifist movement who spent most of his time corresponding by letter with various individuals and groups in the outside world, mostly on pacifist philosophy and logistics and the evils of conscription. After the war, he established a bookstore in Menlo Park, California, which is still there and bears his name.

No. 10 – Had been a student in a Georgia University—enjoyed playing baseball. Raised in the South, but had outgrown southern racial biases.

No. 11 – Of Italian background and from New York City, he was quite sophisticated; an interesting conversationalist and an excellent card player. Think he had gone to Fordham University.

No. 12 – Also of Italian background and from the New York

Many of the conscientious objectors were sent to Newberry to The Upper Peninsula Hospital for the Insane for observation and study, but none were ever admitted for mental illness. George Baird, a Germfask conscientious objector, confided with a sense of humor, "They placed us here because it is close to the excellent hospital in Newberry and because it is near two German prisoners of war camps. Those prisoners are assigned the same doctors as us and they get better medical attention."

Work slowdowns and contrived illness were not the only frustrations employees at the camp had to tolerate. There were numerous other infractions. Two of the barracks housed men who lived more consistently with military regulations. Norman Nelson said that about 20 percent of the men stirred up 90 percent of the trouble. The 20 percent lived in the third barracks. They called it "Tobacco Road" complete with "Toujours Gai Coffee House." This was the barracks of the incorrigibles, and the men who lived there bragged that it was the most publicized barracks of all CPS camps.

All lights were supposed to be out by 10 p.m. They were usually out by midnight in the first two barracks, but in Tobacco Road, they were on all night. Camp officials considered throwing the main electrical switch, but they feared the men would burn candles and start a fire.

The conscientious objectors were responsible for keeping the camp clean, but not surprisingly, given their frequent refusal to work, the camp was declared unsanitary by the Department of Health. Listed among the infractions: the kitchen floors and walls were filthy with grease and dirt, the kitchen storage room was littered with rubbish, garbage cans were unemptied and filthy, and kitchen utensils were washed but exposed to bacteria.

There was also a blatant disregard for rules concerning leave. Regulations required that each man sign out whenever he left camp, stating his destination and expected time of return. From the beginning, the rules were bent for these men. They were allowed to leave camp for short periods of time with no restrictions. As time progressed, only a few men officially bothered to sign out when leaving for longer periods of time; most just came and went as they pleased. A man missing from camp for ten consecutive days was considered Absent Without Leave (AWOL). His name was taken off the roster and given to the federal district attorney in Grand Rapids, Michigan. If he were indicted and convicted of being AWOL, he could be sent to federal prison.

Many of the Germfask men walked out of camp as further protest against the war, knowing they would be imprisoned. In January of 1945, US District Attorney Joseph Deeb reported the last of the fourteen accused of desertion from Camp Germfask had been apprehended and six had been prosecuted.

Following is a breakdown of the available man-days (a unit of one day's work by one man) wasted during the 388 days of the camp's existence. The numbers seem high for a camp that held no more than seventy-five men at one time, but the explanation is simple. One man might be arrested, then released from jail on several different occasions. Some men accused of AWOL returned to camp, claiming they were on furlough, only to walk out again a few days later. The rotating doctors declared 50 percent of all men they examined as well and able to work. The next day, those faking illnesses put themselves back on sick leave and stayed in bed until the doctor returned. It was an endless cycle.

JAIL	**570**
REFUSAL TO WORK	**383**
MISCELLANEOUS	**175**
FURLOUGH	**1,558**
AWOL	**4,971**
SICK	**3,594**

The CO's goal was to publicize their plight. To gain support for their views and express their frustrations, they wrote to government officials, newspapers, and magazines. In addition, they published a weekly newspaper, the *Germfask Newsletter,* and sent copies to other (CPS) camps in hopes of marshaling support for their cause. The newsletters defended their behavior, described daily activities, and reported which fellow COs had been sent to prison.

The letter writing campaign and passive resistance techniques brought national attention to Germfask but no sympathy. Americans, unified in support of the war, saw "Camp Germfask" as a government-protected camp for commies, cowards, and traitors.

A Newberry, Michigan News editorial stated, "The Germfask conchies [COs] are the worst of the breed; tough, lazy and rebellious, those who refuse to observe regulations or respond to disciplinary authority.

The *Escanaba Daily Press* called it "THE ALCATRAZ OF ALL CO CAMPS."

Time magazine's February 1944 issue published an article, "The Tobacco Road Gang," describing the troublemaker's actions.

Members of the three Peace Churches responsible for the camps feared the negative publicity might threaten the special treatment the churches were given under the Selective Service Act of 1940.

The majority of the men at Germfask understood Selective Service regulations for the camps and used that knowledge to work the system to their advantage. They kept the local, state, and federal court system busy. During the camp's thirteen months' existence, they inundated and frustrated the local courts, Michigan's Attorney General, and the District Court of the United States by filing numerous habeas corpus (unlawful detention or imprisonment) cases and appeals. The arrests, suits, and appeals were reported in local newspapers and some larger newspapers. This angered the general public, but it met the conscientious objectors' goals of publicity.

Many peace groups and individuals worked pro bono publico on behalf of conscientious objectors. Frieda Lazarus, a strong and persuasive anti-war activist was an advocate for them. She and her husband Arthur accompanied Albert Einstein as delegates to the World Disarmament Conference in Geneva in 1933. She was a member of the Women's Peace Union and War Resisters League and a founding member of the Metropolitan Board for Conscientious Objectors. Her son Richard was a CO at Germfask. His memoir is later in this book.

DON DEVAULT

Don DeVault brought national attention to Germfask when The *Washington Post* carried an editorial, "The Pangs of Conscience," in November, 1944. DeVault had earned his PhD at Stanford University in California, and at the time of his induction, he was teaching and doing research in physical chemistry at Stanford. He asked the Selective Service Board to classify him IV-E as a conscientious objector. Instead, it gave him a six-month deferment to continue his work. Six months later, his request was again denied and the board gave him a II-B classification (his work was essential to the country). A year later, the board classified him to noncombatant duty in the army (I-A-O), which meant he would be inducted into the armed forces but not carry a gun.

DeVault refused and spent half of an eighteen-month sentence at McNeil Island Federal Prison in the state of Washington. He was released and classified IV-E, his original request. He was sent to Mancos, Colorado CPS, where he dug ditches, picked rocks, and drove trucks for fifty-one hours a week. When he met another chemist in camp, they set up a lab where they did research on molds from which penicillin is produced. DeVault asked for a detached service position to continue his research, but instead, his request got him a transfer to Germfask, where he again set up his lab using the $5 monthly allowance to buy supplies. He appealed again for detached service, but was denied. Instead of reporting to work at the Seney National Wildlife Refuge, he stayed in the dorm and continued his research.

DEVAULT'S LETTER TO GENERAL HERSHEY

Donated by Phyllis Partridge

CPS Camp No. 135
Germfask, Michigan
September 7, 1944

Major General Lewis B. Hershey, Director
Selective Service System
Washington, D.C.

Dear Sir:

I am writing this on the supposition that the Selective Service System desires to place registrants where they can be of greatest service. As you must know, large numbers of conscientious objectors are trained for and desirous of more useful jobs than those to which they are now assigned. In my case, my occupational questionnaire on file with Selective Service shows that I am trained for and experienced in chemical research.

I wish very much to do work of maximum humanitarian benefit. May I ask, therefore, either:

1. That I be allowed immediately to procure and retain a suitable research in a non-profit organization, salary being limited in amount as much as you like, and the location being at a large distance from my home, if you wish, or

2. That I be assigned immediately to do chemical research on antibiotics (penicillin or related substances) under my own direction in the camp to which I am now assigned, in place of the

regular work of this camp? I have, I believe, already gathered sufficient laboratory equipment around my bunk space to accomplish, with luck, a sufficient amount of such research.

May I expect an answer to these two questions within, say, ten days or, if not, shall assume that silence gives consent?

Yours truly,

Don DeVault, assignee

Norman Nelson, the Camp Director, forwarded Don DeVault's letter to General Hershey and received the following reply from Colonel Kosch.

(S.S.S. letterhead)

Mr. Norman Nelson
Camp Director
Civilian Public Service Camp N. 135
Germfask, Michigan

Subject: Don Charles DeVault

Dear Mr. Nelson:

In reply to your letter of September 10, 1944 enclosing a communication from the above-named assignee I wish to state that consideration cannot be given to this at the present time.

Should there be an opening in a guinea pig project at a later date in which this man could be used, his transfer will be given consideration if his behavior and work record is satisfactory. Until such time, he will be maintained on regular project work.

For the Director
Louis F. Kosch
Colonel, Field Artillery
Assistant Director—Camp Operations

Mr. De Vault sent the following letter to Mr. Nelson after Colonel Kosch's reply.

Sept. 27, 1944

Mr. Nelson:

This reply means that I am done with this foolishness. Henceforth I shall be reporting for work on penicillin or related subjects.

Don DeVault

DeVault was arrested for refusing to work. He plead no contest at his trial and was sentenced to three-and-a-half years in federal prison.

CPS Camp No. 135

Dr. Don DeVault in his homemade laboratory, CPS Camp #135, October 27, 1944. - Digital image from the Paul Wilhelm & Jayne Tuttle Wilhelm Collected Papers (CDG-A), Swarthmore College Peace Collection, Swarthmore, Pennsylvania

Corbett Bishop prior to entering Germfask. Partridge Family Collection

CORBETT BISHOP

Corbett Bishop was one of the more publicized COs. His hunger strikes and passive resistance techniques made national headlines with *Life Magazine*'s article and photographs of him being carried into federal court on a stretcher because he was too weak to walk. "He was a leader among "absolutists" in CPS who believed that as some point, law or regulation needed to be breached as a matter of principle on issues of conscience."

Despite what some newspapers reported, Bishop was not a "crackpot." In the 1930s, he served in the United States Armed Forces where he nurtured his convictions that war and the taking of human life are wrong. He became a devoted follower of Mahatma Gandhi and lived according to those convictions.

Bishop enrolled in the University of Wisconsin where he was a graduate student of chemistry. Prior to being inducted into CPS he left the university, moved to New York, and opened a bookstore.

On March 19, 1942, Bishop entered the Patapsco, Maryland CPS camp. After serving three months, he requested a leave because his bookstore business was in foreclosure. When Selective Service did not respond, he began fasting to protest the non-response to his leave and for forcing CPS men to work without pay. The fast lasted forty-four days. Then he was hospitalized and force fed before being transferred to Camp #32 in West Campton, New Hampshire.

One of Bishop's fasts, in sympathy with Gandhi, lasted twenty-one days. He sent pledges to world leaders, including the King of England, Joseph Stalin, Toyohisko Kagawa (a Japanese Christian pacifist, social reformer, and labor activist) Hitler, Mussolini, and a host of other dignitaries.

Bishop went on a thirty-day hunger strike at Germfask and later deserted the camp, knowing he would be arrested.

Next, Bishop protested in various prisons where it is estimated he fasted a total of 426 days, not including the camp fasts. Through various appeals, his case ended up in federal court at Grand Rapids, Michigan. He was sentenced to three-and-a-half years in Michigan's Milan Federal Penitentiary and fined $1,000.00. He was unconditionally paroled from prison six months after the war's end.

GEORGE KYOSHI YAMADA

"While at CPS Camp # 21 at Cascade Locks, Oregon, Mr. Yamada, a Japanese-American, was arrested for insisting upon not sitting in Negro Heaven at the movies. A trumped up charge of battery was made against him in spite of a state law prohibiting racial discrimination." The Selective Service and the War Relocation Authority ordered Mr. Yamada be discharged from CPS so he could be sent to a Japanese internment camp. Camp 21 CO's wrote letters of protest and the men vowed to engage in nonviolent direct action to stop any attempt to remove Yamada from the camp. The following letter was sent to forty CPS camps:

The 200-odd men, who comprise this camp agree in philosophy opposed to race discrimination. Because of our basic belief in full racial equality and our objection to restriction of civil liberties, we have sent the following telegram to Selective Service.

"Feeling great injustice in the evacuation of fellow citizens of Japanese ancestry, enjoying the same constitutional right that we enjoy, we strongly urge the rescinding of the discharge order affecting George Yamada of C.P.S. Camp 21."

The order was rescinded and Selective Service shipped Yamada to Germfask. He and Bjorn Eikrem walked out of Germfask in protest of the entire conscription process. They were arrested and placed in the Kalamazoo County Jail. Bjorn Eikrem's letter of August 2, 2005 describes what happened next:

I worried about him in jail. I was playing pinochle with Hank Nordness, a Norwegian, as a partner. He seemed to be well-known in jail, so I took advantage of our friendship and told him about George. He told me there was an unused cot in his cell. George moved to his cell, and everything went smoothly.

We were shipped to Ashland Prison. One day I was out for our daily exercise and one of the prisoners said to me, "I understand you guys have a Jap in your group. I've never seen a Jap, but I hate those guys." I said, "How do you know if you have never seen one?"

PETTY THEFT

The men showed solidity when a fellow camper was arrested for petty theft, as CO Alfred Partridge explains in a letter:

Right now we are having a difficult time with a court case of a Jehovah's Witness (J. W.) who tried to ship two pairs of GI issue pants home. Olsen (a paid government employee assigned to Camp Germfask for a short stay to investigate the situation) was here, had his box opened, had him arrested, and he is now awaiting trial on a petty larceny charge. We have gotten the boy a lawyer, and we are working on the case, but the boy is of moron level, and can't be counted on to give a good account of himself. There actually is no case, since the boy was going on furlough and had a perfect right to send his pants home to wear, but Olsen pulled his usual blundering tactics. We are worried about the justice in the court, it being a Justice of the Peace Court. We put on a demonstration which caused Nelson (the director) to run for Olsen; we all started returning our

GI issue clothes in protest as being dangerous to keep. Olsen rushed down, threatened and bluffed, bellowed and cursed, and backed down, etc. He said he would have us all prosecuted for disorderly conduct, then said he was issuing orders right then that no one could return his stuff; then he finished up by saying he couldn't stop us. We also wrote out a petition admitting that we had taken GI stuff out of camp often on furlough implying that if the Jehovah's Witness was guilty so were we. It's a clear case of railroading of a boy who was not compos mentis and we are most anxious to stop such a precedent.

The men decided that if their fellow camper was guilty, they all were guilty so they sent the following letter.

TO WHOM IT MAY CONCERN

(Copies to SCHOOLCRAFT COUNTY PROSECUTING ATTORNEY SHEAHAN, JUDGE OF THE COURT AT MANISTIQUE, CAMP DIRECTOR NELSON, REFUGE MANAGER JOHNSON, VICTOR OLSEN, DIRECTOR OF SELECTIVE SERVICE HERSHEY, and Various Newspapers.)

I, an assignee at Civilian Public Service Camp #135 at Germfask, Michigan, hereby certify that I have taken or sent government-issued clothes out of camp for my use during liberty, leave, or furlough, an act similar to that for which Jack Hood is now being held under a charge of theft in the Schoolcraft County Jail at Manistique. The regulation issued to Camp Directors provide: "Work clothing will be considered suitable for all occasions, or privately owned clothing may be worn when off duty...Assignees will be allowed to bring to camp and wear their own civilian clothing during non-working hours and while away from camp on liberty, leave, or furlough."

Dated, July 31, 1944.

Signed:

Daniel B. Dingman	*Jack Kendre*
Gerald F. Dingman	*Joe Watkins*
Douglas Galbraith	*Joseph Martin*
Curtis Besinger	*John Meneyes*

Morris Horowitz	*Sol Gadol*
Andy Hall	*David J. Miller*
Arden D. Bode	*William G. Goudy*
George Baird	*Richard Lazarus*
Paul J. Browder	*Alfred E. Partridge*
Fred C. Lupo	*Rodney C. Owen*
Claude R. Shattuck	*George F. Foil*
Bill Hordinski	*Bjorn Eikrem*
Walter Ness	*D. E. Kauble*
Edmund Curtis	*Calvin C. Pope Jr.*
Donald H. Burton	*George Yamanda*
Harvey S. Smith	*Purcell Bensen*
Frank W. Hatfield	

MARVIN COOK CASE

Marvin Cook, a twenty-one-year-old conscientious objector, also received ample newspaper coverage. He was arrested for giving false information when he applied for a Michigan trapping license. The store clerk doubted his eligibility for obtaining the permit so she sent him to Mr. Derwin, a local game warden. Mr. Derwin told him he must be a resident of Michigan for six months before he could apply for the license. Cook went back to the store and bought his trapping license. Cook appeared in his own defense and stated he had not realized he had resided in the state for only five months and he had no intention of giving false information. Mr. Derwin testified that Cook had merely asked him what constituted legal residence requirements to obtain the license, not whether he (Cook) were eligible. He was found guilty and appealed his case. Mr. John Bratten, a Lansing attorney, represented him. Without notifying Bratten, Judge Rummels ordered the case from Schoolcraft County to neighboring Luce County. Cook was sentenced to thirty days plus a forty-dollar fine or forty days in jail. He was taken back to Schoolcraft County and placed in solitary confinement by order of the court.

Cook's fellow conscientious objectors were angry that they were not allowed to speak with him. They sent a letter to Congressman Bradley on

January 18, 1945, asking him for support in Cook's case. They were not concerned about the forty dollars, but they were concerned that he had been denied his civil rights.

Bradley published the COs letter in the Manistique and Newberry newspapers along with his reply comparing these unruly men to the responsible Mennonite conscientious objectors and accusing them of making a mockery of democracy with their money, highfalutin lawyers, and backing by the American Civil Liberties Union. Both papers' headlines read, "*TOO DAMN LAZY TO WORK OR FIGHT.*"

Keeping up the pressure, the conscientious objectors released an editorial in the Manistique paper on the same date as Bradley's reply. They said they had no money and Bratten had paid Cook's fine out of his own pocket. The letter to the editor went on to say their objection to war was not necessarily based on religious beliefs but that they were sincere. They begged for tolerance and understanding.

The letter, however, did not bring tolerance and understanding; it only added to the public's resentment.

ATTEMPTED LYNCHING

Sunday, July 2, 1944

The following document was provided by Phyllis Partridge. It was typed and handed out to campers at Germfask and sent to other conscientious objectors camps.

Violence Used on COs at Newberry, Michigan

On Sunday, the second of July, 1944, a group of COs from Germfask CPS Camp #135 went on a short excursion to the nearby town of Newberry, Michigan. This is a small town of about 2,000 population; its chief industry consisting of sawmills. We arrived in a canvas-covered, stake-bodied Forestry truck, somewhat resembling a covered wagon. The truck was conspicuous and almost all of the citizens knew we came to town on some Sundays.

For about two hours, the sixteen COs wandered about the streets, ate in the cafes, and had a bottle of beer or two in the local taverns. They were all waiting for the seven o'clock opening of the movie.

During the two hours, there had been some unpleasantness shown toward some of them; a few had been told by a large lumberjack to get out of town. This man had obviously been drinking heavily so no great attention was paid to his threats. The actual trouble started in three different sectors of the town at about the same time. One boy, who was reading in the cab of the truck, parked on a side street, had been threatened by a coast guards-man and a civilian. He had talked to them in the truck, but they insisted that he get out of the truck and start walking out of town; this he did. Two other boys who were standing in front of the theater had been threatened and forcibly escorted toward the edge of town but managed to get to the police station instead, and notified the police of the trouble brewing. An-other CO, having seen a mob around the truck, notified the police.

In a tavern, the four COs had entered for a glass of beer, seated them-selves, and had not yet been waited on, when the big lumberjack and the coast guardsman mentioned above, and four or five others, came over to them. The big fellow demanded to know where they had come from. They didn't tell at once, and he then said he knew they were "dirty yellow bel-lies from Germfask and that they had better get out of the bar and out of town immediately." The boys put up no resistance but walked unhurriedly to the door; the last two were severely kicked several times by one or more of these men before they reached the door to the street. They turned toward town, intending to round up the rest of their fellow campers, one of whom was the driver with the keys to the truck, but the group of huskies forced them to go directly to the truck. By the time they reached it, a crowd of about fifteen were gathered around them. They were kicked again as they clambered into the back of the truck. By this time, a crowd was gathering fast and was shouting and cursing the boys. The leaders of the mob were big working men well on their way to intoxication who kept up a steady stream of insults. The four COs asked these leaders to come into the truck and talk the matter over. Four of them climbed in, and for a short time, the COs tried to explain why they wouldn't fight for their country. But they were not given much chance since all the while they were interrupted by oaths, curses, and threats. By this time, a crowd of about sixty people had gathered outside and were shouting, "Lynch them! Throw them in the river! Pull out his beard!" (One of the men, Al Partridge, seemed to be singled out for particular hatred because of his beard.)

At this moment, the large lumberjack made one of the men get out with him and go in search of the truck driver and the rest of the campers. Also, the man with the beard was commanded to come to the back of the truck and tell the crowd why he was a yellow CO. This he did, sitting on the rear of the truck with his feet hanging over the back. He tried to talk calmly to the crowd (there were nearly a hundred by now) more in the hope of restraining their violence than enlightening them. Although he may have succeeded in gaining a little time before they broke into violence, he was so out-shouted by the threatening mob that most of its meaning was lost. After he had been talking about ten minutes, another of the COs came up to find out what was going on and immediately a drunken coast guards-man started to swing at him, landing a few ineffectual blows before he was restrained by some of the crowd who seemed afraid he would get into trouble with the Navy. This CO was kicked violently several times as he climbed into the truck. By this time, the mob was beginning to demand ac-tion and starting to pull the man who had been speaking off the truck when the lumberjack with his hostage and another CO came up. The truck driver fortunately arrived at this time also. They jumped into the truck, and just as several of the crowd started to climb in after them, the driver got under way and left the crowd behind.

It was now necessary to round up the other COs. They gathered several up as they drove to the edge of town, then spent a few minutes deciding how best to find the others. At this moment, the State Police car drove up and followed the truck back into town, where they collected the rest of the boys without further interference.

ADDENDUM

Four days later, the State Police came to the camp and talked to the director. They repeated what the coast guardsman had told them. They believed the conscientious objectors in the tavern had been drinking and laughing loudly; they had insulted his uniform, and he had knocked one of them down. The man had refused to get up, so they threw the conscientious objectors out.

One of the campers attempted to tell the police the actual occurrence, but the police did not believe him. They stated that all conscientious objectors were nothing but draft dodgers and should be sentenced to five years in prison, and if they ever returned to Newberry, the police would make it a point to be out of town.

End of story

BANNED

Public resentment was becoming very common. Manistique citizens resented the men being driven into town in a government truck when gas rationing was on. They threw garbage at the truck. They did not want them walking down their streets.

The conscientious objectors had been banned from Newberry in 1944 following the flare-up between them and residents, and now, in January of 1945, Judge William Sheahan banned them from Manistique. They were not allowed to visit the city, pass through Manistique on foot, or hitch-hike to destinations beyond Manistique. They were only permitted to pass through the city in automobiles or other vehicles. Police Chief Elmer Anderson announced that any conchies found in the city would be immediately arrested. The following Sunday, a conscientious objector was picked up and lodged in the county jail until officers from camp came to return him to Germfask.

In a letter to camp director Norman Nelson, published in the *Manistique Pioneer Tribune* on January 26, 1945, Judge Sheahan stated, "Public opinion has reached such a stage that I am fearful that violence will ensue if you continue to permit members of your camp to visit this city. Such a state of unrest exists to create an emergency…violence did not come from a hoodlum element but from solid citizens among whom were trustees of a church."

Clyde Strassler, a Manistique resident and member of the First Baptist Church recalls "Several elders blocked the door and refused to let them in. The community didn't like them being around the young girls while our young boys were at war."

COMPLETE CHAOS

On February 4, 1945, the *Escanaba Daily Press* carried a front-page story headlined "SABOTAGE IN THE KITCHEN." Camp manager Earl R. Waltz (Waltz took over as manager when Reverend Osborne quit) described the mess in the kitchen—a 100-pound bag of kidney beans was broken and scattered, three jars of mustard were broken, which saturated thirty pounds of baking powder; rice, prunes, and apricots were mixed together; two lightbulbs were smashed; two oven doors were removed but found the next day. Some tableware also disappeared.

Many national newspapers picked up on the story. Below is the February 6, 1945 night edition of the *Detroit Times* headlined in bold red print, "War Objectors Mutiny" and described "Intellectuals in Revolt."

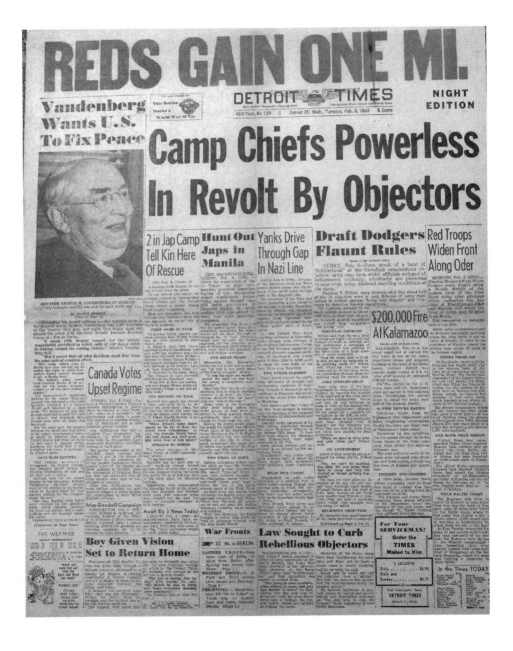

The *Detroit Free Press*, reported the story in its February 6, 1945, night edition.

War Objectors Mutiny
Seney Camp Intelllectualts' in Revolt

Special to the Detroit Times

SENEY, MICH., Feb. 6—A large group of conscientious objectors assigned to the large wild life refuge near Seney were reported in open mutiny today against camp officials and government restrictions.

The mutineers, according to Director Norman V. Nelson, were led by a group of "intellectuals" and college professors who have advised the 74 objectors not to work or obey any orders.

Nelson admitted that the insurgent objectors already have seized and destroyed a large quantity of foodstuffs and that some of them have openly defied the authorities to compel them to work.

Nelson has appealed to the FBI, which he said will make an immediate complete investigation of the camp.

"The majority of these men," Nelson said, **"are highly educated. They resent the restrictions the government has placed on them. We have had trouble with them before, but conditions at present call for action."**

The director admitted that the majority of the 74 men have been working eight and one-half hours a day and have given little trouble. Others, he said, refuse to perform any sort of labor.

The men are given an allowance of $5 and two and one-half days furlough each month.

Five of the objectors were given prison sentences several weeks ago for refusing to work. The men are mostly employed on the maintenance work.

Leonard Lewis, a CO, whose interview follows, stated the following:

"The newspapers made it look like we were as bad as the enemy. I wanted to call the *Press* and tell them the story was totally false, but we weren't allowed to leave camp and we weren't allowed to use the camp phone. We didn't even know to what they were referring."

In a 1989 interview with the author, Mr. Nelson, the camp director, stated, "I did not tell any reporter there was mutiny at Germfask; I did not tell any reporter there was a rebellion at Germfask. The reporter lied."

In an effort to stop rumors and ease tensions, Nelson issued a public denial that rioting and mutiny had occurred. That denial appeared on February 9, in the *Mining Journal,* an Upper Peninsula paper based in Marquette, Michigan. It was the only newspaper that printed his statement.

Meanwhile, rumors of a riot were circulating and the FBI and Selective Service were under pressure to do something about the situation.

'Co' Camp
Riot Reports 'Utterly False'

MANISTIQUE, Feb 8- Terming "utterly fantastic", the news releases concerning Camp Germfask given screamer headlines in many metropolitan dailies throughout the country last Tuesday, Norman V. Nelson, the camp manager, "denied that any rioting or mutiny among the college professors, intellectuals or lowbrows had as yet occurred at the camp".

Nelson confirmed the report that members of the FBI and army officials were investigating conditions, but denied that they had come because of any outbreak in the camp. He added that this investigation had been considered for a long time, but that it had probably been hastened by local publicity protesting against the lack of authority invested in camp officials and public indignation resulting from these disclosures.

C.A. Brown, one of the FBI investigators, confirmed Nelson's statement. The articles recently published in the Escanaba Daily Press "certainty started something," he said.

The results of the investigation and the recommendations made have not as yet been made public. Nelson intimated however, that ways and means would be found to put the loafers and trouble makers to work out in the woods at tasks which will keep them busy and their minds engaged with other things than self-pity and ways of flaunting authority.

Not communicating with Nelson and unaware of his public denial, government officials continued to investigate the situation. Colonel Lewis F. Kosch, at Selective Service Headquarters, Washington, DC, issued a statement on February 12, 1945, that he had reported the alleged insurrection, treason, and destruction of government property to the FBI office, but that the FBI did not investigate or prosecute because of the trivial character of the violations. The FBI responded to Kosch's statement, saying it was false, that it investigated all cases, but it would do no further investigations of the Germfask conscientious objectors until it was directed to do so by United States Attorney Deeb.

The following day, February 13, 1945, FBI files report that the FBI had heard rumors of the riot and was trying to "get a line on it," but up to that date, it had not been requested to investigate.

At 6:18 p.m. on that same day, a special agent reported that there was no "active insurrection but that on the night of January 30, 1945, ten to fifteen objectors had broken into the food stores and damaged considerable amounts of supplies." He went on to say it would be "difficult to prove destruction of Government property against the conscientious objectors involved."

On that same evening at 11:25 p.m., an agent stated in a written memo that the camp authorities had no information of a threatened insurrection and that no agents should be sent into camp "while the situation is as it is."

The cost of the damage to food and property was $25.00. The case was closed and placed in the hands of CPS Camp administration rather than for prosecution by the courts.

A *Newberry News* editorial on February 9, 1945 recommended "a woods foreman of the old type would clean up that mess so quick it would make your head swim."

An editorial in the *Chicago Tribune* in March, 1945 called it "*THE GERMFASK FOLLIES*" and recommended that military be dispatched to control "one-third of the men who have been involved in work slowdowns, malingering and other obstructionist tactics for some time."

LEONARD LEWIS

May 27, 1980 Phone Interview

Leonard Lewis at Lapine, Oregon. Vincent Beck collection

"I figured out the statistics that the average army man had an eighth-grade education and the average CPS man had a second-year college education. This information was sent to the federal judge to be used in the Corbett Bishop trial.

"The men at Germfask were very intelligent. One man continued his experimental research in cancer, another continued with his bio-chemical research. He was trying to determine whether there was a physical reason for some men being homosexual. They brought their lab equipment with them and kept right on working.

"We had only a few footlockers in the camp. The administration said they would try to make us some. I told them that if they would give me two days to get the materials, we'd make better lockers and make them faster. In two days, we had a big pile of lumber. I said, 'Come back in two days and the lockers will be done.' They said they never saw a group of men that would study a problem and then do it right like we did. The CCCs had everything they owned in one suitcase. We had shelves, books, and microscopes.

"One man was drafted who spoke only Spanish. We taught him English and how to read and write both Spanish and English. That's the kind of men we were, but they called us the incorrigibles.

"We had to cut down trees in the winter and go back in the summer and cut off the four-foot stumps. They'd give us an axe and say, 'Cut down this tree.' We'd say, 'What's an ax? How do you use it?' etc.

"Dave Miller, one of the campers, and I were sent to Milwaukee for a physical. We found that we had several hours before our bus left to take us back to Germfask, so we decided to do some sightseeing. When the commander asked our guards where we were, they told him we went sightseeing. He told them we should be under guard at all times. He was afraid we would disappear or do something to bring embarrassment to him. Dave's wife and baby were staying in Germfask, so he had no intention of running away, nor did I. They finally found us walking along the street. They told us to get into the car. We got into the car and then spent the rest of the day with them. We told them about our views and feelings, and when we said our goodbyes, they said they respected us. After they got to know us, they liked us.

"General Hershey sent me a letter asking that I consider being reclassified. He could have found me an easy office job. I refused, of course.

"I have no regrets. I would make the same decision today. I could never kill anyone just because someone told me to kill. No one could make me kill another person because he wanted it done. A business competitor accused me falsely, and this caused me great frustration. I had to get legal counsel, my reputation was marred, and I did feel like killing him. I didn't, but if I would have, it would have been my decision, not someone else's.

"Intelligence was involved in my decision, but it was guts, mostly just plain guts that made me stick to my decision. It was a hard decision. Many families were split. The wife, girlfriend, or parents did not always agree. Some brothers went into the service, and some became conscientious objectors. It was not easy.

DAN DINGMAN LETTERS
Dan Dingman Collection

Following are excerpts from letters Dan wrote to his brother from CPS 135 in Germfask.

Wednesday, 11/15/44

...There isn't even any such thing as a project anymore, even in name. Still no government cook, and the boys have charge in the kitchen. Of about eighty men in camp (new ones coming all the time—mostly from other camps and one parolee), ten cooks, eight to ten are KPs (kitchen patrol), all sorts of firemen, wood carriers, handy-men about camp, librarians, night-watchmen, office men, etc., plenty of SQs (sick quarters); Nick, Morris, Frank, and I on the penal crew cutting fire wood, with Dave Miller sneaking in on our crew, so it has actually settled down to a pure fight for survival—and we don't keep very far ahead of the fuel consumption at that.

We have spent the last few project days building us a snug little room above the stove in the old lumber camp, and outside we have hung a large sign reading "WK of NATL IMP, - LTD. Refuge #1". (Work of National Importance, Limited, at Refugee Camp #1) That is located about fifty yards from the woodpile, but we very seldom even visit that, and I have read at least seven different books while on that project.

There are many weather days, and if—by some chance—there is a mistake made, they decide to go to the first-aid meeting, sit around a half hour or so with the fellows, and then tune in on the football games.

The morning routine is simple; work call is about eight, at which time Doug lightly taps you and says, "Work call, everybody out." Until then, the only two in the dorm up are he and Gerry, who have already had their coffee and have it ready for the others who want it. Many of the fellows get up at Doug's call, though only Doug, Nick, Morris, Dave, and I go to [a] project from our dorm. We usually just pick up a hunk of bread and jam and eat it on the way to work in the truck.

Sunday is the one day when most of the fellows eat breakfast—when they get up around ten to eleven, and what a meal that is! Either fresh fruit, or canned grapefruit, orange juice, etc. Then cereal—Shredded Wheat, Corn Flakes, or what have you; and after that, perhaps pancakes, or toasted cheese sandwiches, sausage, and/or eggs as you like them—all this is in the dorm at the Toujours Gai, of course—most of us have no idea what, if anything, goes on in the dining hall at any time in the morning.

The kitchen is really a mess! Walz gave up on the idea of locks, and everything is perfectly open except for the jams, sugar, eggs, and other things he keeps at his quarters and doles out on occasion. It is a common evening occurrence for us to go over to stock the Toujours Gai with cereals, bread, butter, crackers, spreads, eggs, oranges, milk, raisins, and whatever else they have that we need. We also have plenty of occasion to use the fund in the orange jar on the Toujours Gai table for replenishing our supply from downtown, since the kitchen cupboard is often bare. In the evening, you can usually find several fellows over there cooking steaks, or frying eggs, and eating cereal when the other food has run out. I honestly don't know how the cooks manage to get enough stuff together for meals every day, and they don't do too well at that.

Sunday evening is a cafeteria meal, at best, and every now and then the same thing happens at other meals. Last night, there just wasn't any service, nor any tableware out, so everyone mobbed the kitchen. What a mess! Everyone ate out of the first thing they could lay their hands on—grabbing the chops right from the stove, getting out their own milk, bread, etc. and paying no attention to anyone else. At a recent vote in the dining hall, only two fellows were against letting fellows take things out of the kitchen whenever they wanted to, but things have really gone pretty far! So far, the administration hasn't said or done anything about it, but they seldom appear at meals, anyhow.

We had the FBI man around for three days, after which he was joined by two more, and now all are gone. We don't know why they came. They questioned Leonard Lewis about some property stolen and Gooky about forcing the lock to get out some food needed by cooks while Walz was out of camp.

Andy Hall was voluntarily sent to the state mental hospital at Newberry for examination, but returned today after about three days. He was planning to stay a couple of weeks, but said he couldn't stand it. And that's all the news from here....

12/27/44

...Doug came back from Chicago after nine days AWOL, so we had the Toujours Gai operating full swing long before Christmas. Neubrand was picked up in Pittsburg, Ohio, and is out on bail as far as I know. Horowitz headed for Washington and probably has been picked up there; but it was Partridge who got the dirty deal. We don't have the story straight yet, but he was picked up, and is now out on bail. Meanwhile, his wife has been picked up on a charge of desertion by the Chicago police, and the kid is in an orphanage. Many of Al's letters were also taken, and they have been considering making a sedition charge against him. I wish those guys would write more often so we could keep in closer touch with them.

I guess you hear about Bish [Corbett Bishop] and the others in Grand Rapids. Heilsler (attorney) of Chicago decided to help out on those cases, and seems to be doing a good job. They have been postponed to the fifth of January again, and we don't know what will happen then. Bish refused to accept bail, and would not promise to return for trial or give any security of any kind. He would not even answer when the judge tried to make some sort of a deal with him to release him until his trial. So finally the judge just let him go without any bond of any kind. Bish got up, said, "Thank you," and walked out of the court. They'll have to pick him up all over again for the trial.

Ralph Pulliam was picked up here by the marshal a few weeks back. He is the one who turned in all his GI [government-issued clothes] when Hood was picked up. Since then, he has been reporting to work every day, and then saying he couldn't go out because of insufficient clothing. He claims they should give a cash allowance to buy things with, as the rules allow. The charge against him is failure to report for work of national importance at CPS 135. He was taken to Marquette and arraigned and is now out on bail. He should come up for trial at Sault Ste. Marie in January, but since his is the only case on their docket, they aren't going to go to the expense of having a session then; so he will be out until the April court session in Marquette.

Mike Cimbanin got his 4-F two weeks back. It was about time! We had a real old celebration when he left—the first good party I've seen since Mancos. There was a case of soda pop, a bottle of whiskey, and several bottles of wine we were storing for Christmas, and they all went along with the food that happened to be around, and, of course, plenty of singing, joking, smoking, and even a nice long Conga line led by Hatfield.

About that time, I also spent my first weekend in jail. It was this-a-way: Nelson had canceled all weekend leaves because a couple of boys smashed a crate of rotten cold-storage eggs. Well, I and Rev. Curtis (an interesting "character" who came here this summer from detached service) decided to go to Manistique anyhow. We bummed down and spent the night in a hotel. In the morning, we went to church, and then stopped at the Eat Shop for a bite of lunch before bumming back. One of the state police spotted us there and wanted to know where we were from. We told him, and when he found we didn't have passes, he said he'd have to pick us up. I asked why, and he mumbled something about a federal law, and said that all police in the Upper Peninsula had orders to pick up any conscientious objectors without passes. He was very nice, though, and went to the counter and had some coffee while waiting for us to finish eating. Then he took us to the county sheriff's place. There he asked a mess of questions, and then asked us to step upstairs. Only then did we realize we were in jail, and he slid the bolt quietly behind us. The sheriff was not so polite; fed us lousy food, refused to tell us the charges, wouldn't let us use a phone, and didn't even give us clean sheets for the dirty double bed. On Monday, they switched us to the cell-block downstairs where they also had kept Dicky Lazarus overnight, but they still refused to tell us anything. Late that afternoon, the director came down and they released us. We haven't bothered to kick about it, though, because we already have so much trouble to straighten out in the county court. Incidentally, we all got AWOL for our time in jail.

A lot of RTWs (Refusal to Work) are also being issued lately—rather indiscriminately, too. Doug got one for last Sunday, and I just received two for days when I was SQ and had been treated by the Doc. At present, I think I have something like four RTWs and sixteen AWOLs to my credit—at least. I just figured it out that I will have exactly one day of furlough coming on March 9th, 1946—a year from this coming spring, if I'm a good boy between now and then.

Lewis and Hawking arrived safely from La Pine a while back; and Kekoni (or whatever his name is) came a few days later.

The doctor here is on the rampage again. Practically half the camp is reporting temperatures, and he is trying to find out what causes it. In Browder's case, he found he had strep throat, and he has sent specimens from several of us out to be examined for the same thing. He also checked the water and milk supplies. And he insists on taking temperature himself, because he wants to see whether we're pulling any tricks. One day recently, he took mine six times, and it gradually rose from 97 to 99 degrees. I haven't any more idea than he has why it was because I don't have a fever, and only went over to report a sore back. Then he checked the kitchen, and has bawled out both administration and campers for the unsanitary conditions there. That can't cause all the trouble, though, because on a typical day like today, no one from this dorm went to breakfast, and only four to dinner. We survive mainly on stuff sent to us, and what we buy uptown out of the Toujours Gai Fund.

Kehl and Lazarus are both AWOL at present, and it is anybody's guess whether either will decide to stay out.

Outside of that, things have been fairly quiet around here lately.

3/23/45

I'll give you what I can recall of what has been going on here in the past month or so.

On the publicity angle, did you see the article on "The Tobacco Road Gang" in *Time* magazine for Feb. 19 (also in letters to the editor, Mar. 19)? That was sort of a combination of the stuff from the Upper Peninsula newspapers and *Detroit Free Press*. More, of course, has been appearing regularly in both presses—some of the regular stuff, and some almost decent articles. I shan't bother to enclose any of them because this doggone thing is going to be bulky enough when I get through anyhow. However, I am sticking in portions of the Congressional record for January 30 and 31, because they are Bradley's speeches [Congressman Fredrick Van Ness Bradley, US Republican representative from Michigan's 11 congressional district] about us, and are really dirty. Just before he went home, the *Chicago Tribune* sent one of its reporters up, and he gathered enough "material" for a series of five articles—some of which quote quite freely from Nick, my brother, and myself, not very accurately, either. Naturally they, too, have printed a few letters to the editor on the subject.

Germfask also joined the movement some time ago by circulating a petition to keep us out of town—sixty people signed, one fellow twice. It doesn't mean much apparently, just a gesture. Those who want to still go to town with no more trouble than before, though there isn't much there to go for. Many who signed are just as friendly as before, including two of the foreman—one of whom has Lang's wife staying at his home. Others who signed come to the movies with no signs of hostility. It's hard to figure out. Apparently those who started it and circulated it mean something, but the rest just signed because of local pressure.

We are having trouble again with government employees. Among other things, we just took on another foreman, but I don't see where they're going to use him. Nice fellow, and local talent like the rest of 'em. Our army doc., Pintozz, got out in January, possibly (according to rumor) because he resented the fact that no one paid any attention to his recommendations. Another army doc. Davis, took over. He was a worse mental case than the worst of the men. Finally pulled out in favor of an old civilian gent, Powers, who seems quite friendly, though I know nothing of his ability yet. Rather quietly, and without any explanation, Camp Manager Walz left about the first of the month. In his place came an ex-serviceman, individualist named Voelker. I didn't have much to do with him, but others said he was something of a pain merely because he talked so much. Obviously wanted to be friendly and do the best by us. The day Gerald and I came back, we learned he had tendered his resignation, in which he explains that he can no longer take part in the administration of such a slave-system. The resignation was picked up by both AP and UP and got good publicity, including at least one radio broadcast. He was finally persuaded to stay over the weekend when his successor resigned without showing up. Newest at the job is Hutt, another local fellow who looks like he may be okay.

FBI blew in again Monday (two agents, Brown and Thompson, each in a separate car). Interviewed quite a few of us on Tuesday and Wednesday. Object: who broke the mustard jars ($5 damage at most) almost two weeks ago. Actually, most of us really don't know, but it doesn't seem possible they could really expect us to tell even if we did. It seems awfully fishy for them to spend so much time on such a little thing, but apparently, they're looking for a scapegoat for publicity. Definitely didn't seem interested in anything else we had to offer. Don't know what they learned; gone now.

It is reported that a Legionnaire and Congressman were in the office yesterday—maybe, nothing happened. Bradley and a few other congressmen, along with prosecutor Sheahan, did pay us a visit sometime in February. Didn't stop, though; just breezed through. The Congressman was at Blaney Park at a conference with regard to fisheries on the Great Lakes.

Cook case was automatically closed when Marvin's time was up. Sheahan had promised to send Bratten necessary facts for the appeal, but backed out. At the last minute, Bratten tried to get a Habeas Corpus to get Marvin out pending appeal. No luck. Hood case still hanging in mid-air. Still no trial, no bail, and Hood's possessions are still in Manistique.

Rumors are still high on what is going to happen next. Very latest is a renewal of the rumor that we are all going to ship back to Mancos. (Mancos reports extensive cleaning-up and preparations for eight new men.) Rumor is generally pretty highly doubted around here. After several weeks, we are beginning to wonder whether anything at all will happen as a result of publicity. A few weeks ago, personal files of thirteen of us (Dingman, Fiore, Flowers, Kekoni, Lazarus, L. Lewis, Lupo, Migliorino, Miller, Galbraith, R. Riddle, Stackton, Welch) spent several days on Nelson's desk. Rumors started again. All thirteen were requested to take physical exams while second army doc was here. Some of us did, others refused. Nick finally decided to a few days later and went back. Civilian doc said, "Sorry," but Nelson had gone to Grand Rapids (also to Washington, we know) and taken the files with him. The list seems strange, we can't figure it out; and now after some time, we are beginning to wonder whether it meant anything. Five best guesses were (1) releases; (2) return to draft board for reclassification, perhaps insincere; (3) prosecution on some charges; (4) transfer to a new unit; (5) transfer and dispersion by sending to existing units and detached service. Take your pick.

Another fellow, Louis Beyreis, just got his 4-F, makes eight to date (Mendro, Hordinskim Smith, Hall, Ness*, Cimbanin, Hughes*, and Beyreis—asterisk indicates that they had petition for Writ of Habeas Corpus. At present six others (Fiore, Kehl, Fell, Borglund, Wesner, Cordell) have petitions in for Writs. All on medical, and other grounds; no action yet.

Maybe I can catch you up a bit on the walk-out and court situation a bit. Here's the score as far as I know.

Stang	4-F
Calef	4-F
Matton	not tried yet, probably sometime this month.
Banaszak	3 yrs. prison
Pope	3 yrs. prison
Burton	3 yrs. prison
Bishop	4 yrs. prison and $1,000
	(got plenty of publicity, too, not all bad)
Eikrem	3 ½ yrs. prison
DeVault	3 ½ yrs. prison
Pulliam	to be tried this month
Partridge	decision coming on April 2nd.
Neubrand	" " " "
Horowitz	" " " "
Stokes	3 yrs. prison
Fogarty	trial in Marquette next month
Yamada	decision coming on April 2nd.
Bode	" " " "
Owen	" " " "
Hopkins	" " " "

CAMP GERMFASK CLOSED

Camp Germfask opened in May, 1944 and remained open until June, 1945. Because of the administration's lack of control and the residents of Germfask and surrounding community's extreme hostility toward the men, it became necessary to transfer the conscientious objectors out of the area. Selective Service considered moving them to Isle Royale in Lake Superior (a national park) where they would be unable to have any contact with the outside world except through government channels. Because of harsh winter weather conditions and the possibility of not being able to get to the island for emergencies, however, Selective Service opted to transfer them to a remote camp in the mountains near Minersville, California.

Shortly before the camp closed, Selective Service discharged and reclassified many of the assignees. The government believed it had eliminated most of the nonviolent recalcitrants. Many were examined by a special medical advisory board and reclassified IV-F (physically, mentally, or morally unfit) while others were given discharges due to age and length of service. The remainder of the men were sent to Minersville, California CPS 148, which opened in June of 1945.[19]

DISCONTENTMENT AND RESISTANCE GROWS[20]

Following V-E Day, May 18, 1945, a time signifying victory in Europe by the Allied forces, the problem of order and discipline in the civilian population increased throughout the nation. The November 18, 1945 issue of the *Washington Post* reported fears of a breakdown in manpower at a national level. Shipbuilder Henry J. Kaiser of Richmond, California, reported to the President of the United States that in a three-month period, 26,000 men left their shipyard jobs "to get ahead of what they believe will be a rush for peacetime employment. They didn't even bother to ask for a certificate of availability which would permit them to change jobs."

19   U.S. Department of Justice, Washington, DC. FBI Report. Confidential Conference Regarding Closing of Camp Germfask. February 10, 1945, file number 61-11043-7.
20   Facts in this chapter are taken from Selective Service System. *Conscientious Objection: Special Monograph*. Vol 1. No. 11. Washington, DC: Government Printing Office, 1950. p. 241-249.

The war ended officially on September 2, 1945, but all conscripted men, both in the armed forces and CPS, were drafted for the duration of the war plus six months. Their ages ranged from eighteen to fifty year olds. The war department continued to induct men until October 15, 1946, and it didn't release all inductees until August 30, 1947. Discontentment was spreading throughout all branches of the armed forces. The war was over; men wanted to go home.

The CPS men were emulating what was happening on a national level and the problems that surfaced at Germfask were only a forewarning of dissatisfaction that was to occur in the total CPS program.

In the summer of 1945, when the first camp newsletter at Minersville (written and published by Gerald Dingman and his transferred crew from Germfask) was distributed, it became evident to Selective Service the trouble had not ended. An editorial by an assignee asked the administration to resign from the slavery system. The "Camp Germfask" tactics continued, and officials were unable to get the men to complete work projects. Eventually, the foremen didn't bother to tell a man to work; they merely told him to report to his work station.

A series of acts of sabotage began. Equipment was destroyed, and finally, the mess hall and a storage building were burned down. The government investigated to determine whether an organized movement of open rebellion might break out. They discovered their fears were unfounded; organized resistance never existed, and the sabotage was probably the work of no more than two men.

Unrest was beginning to brew among the general population of CPS men and the problems of order and discipline accelerated. In December of 1945, *THE CPS-GI*, the Mancos mimeographed newsletter of the uncooperative group stated, "as CPS throughout the nation grinds on its last legs, I feel sure that general unrest and dissatisfaction will break out into active nonviolent noncooperation, a fitting end to CPS." They sent a copy of this letter to all CPS camps.

The first and only organized attempted resistance in a CPS church camp occurred in Glendora, California. It began in February of 1946. A group calling themselves "The Irresponsibles" published a letter in the camp newspaper that explained techniques of resistance to be used to make CPS an unsuccessful experiment in conscription:

1. We can refuse to take responsibility for the project; that is the job of

the camp administrator and his aides—they get paid for it—let's not help them evade the obligations of their positions. We can only take orders.

2. We can slow down and do as little work as possible; we can at least keep the project part of CPS from operating smoothly. The merits of this method are that a few men can start a slow-down, that it can bog a project, and that it is not illegal. Generally those who slow down should be on the project, not in administrative positions, overhead, or positions of responsibility.

3. We can refuse to work; it is rumored that this is illegal—but it is sometimes necessary to break the law. The project suffers when men do not work. The primary advantage over the slow-down method is that the individual has more time to spend in a constructive manner.

4. We can walk out of CPS; this method enables a man to personally escape the evils of CPS. To render CPS ineffective and to be socially worthwhile, a walk-out must be done by 99.44/100 percent of the men.

5. We can practice sabotage. This method of resistance is advocated by many pacifists and has been practiced in some CPS camps. A program of sabotage for success must have clearly defined goals and close organization.

On March 1, 1946, the church-sponsored Glendora camp was changed to a government camp.

Unrest continued at Glendora, and on April 24, 1946, Selective Service identified two men it believed were members of the Irresponsibles who wrote the letter. They were given orders to transfer to the "New Camp Germfask" in Minersville, California. They refused to transfer and were reported to an attorney for prosecution. Later that day, twenty-five assignees at Glendora refused to work in support of the two men and what they termed "arbitrary" action by the administration in ordering the transfer.

During meetings with the Department of Justice, the Selective Service asked for a speedy prosecution of the Glendora men, but the Department was hesitant to prosecute. The situation was reported to the Attorney General, but he advised that prosecution be delayed.

By May 18, 1946, eighty-two assignees from Glendora had refused to work for over fifteen days. That day, six men were finally identified as ringleaders and arrested, but it did not deter the others. The United States Attorney General began to take the necessary steps to prosecute these men, but he was advised by the Department of Justice not to prosecute until a full investigation by the FBI was completed. On May 27, 1946, fifty-one more men were arrested. The trials were not held until March of 1947. Of those men arrested, many requested to be returned to work and charges were dropped. Thirty more cases were dropped to speed up the court process and twenty-one of the group of violators were prosecuted and convicted in a Federal court in Los Angeles.

On May 1, 1946, forty men at CPS No. 46 in Big Flats, New York, engaged in refusal-to-work demonstrations. Selective Service wanted to arrest the men, but the Department of Justice in Washington ordered it to arrest only those who could be identified as troublemakers and ringleaders. After this order was made public, only six men continued to refuse to work, and they were arrested, tried, and convicted in a Federal court at Buffalo.

At the same time, the number of men resisting in other camps was increasing daily. Unrest was reported in CPS camps in Cascade Locks, Oregon; Three Rivers, California; Mesa, Arizona; Philadelphia, Pennsylvania; Gatlinburg, Tennessee; and Bowie, Maryland.

Sympathetic demonstrations at other camps were also held, but the men eventually returned to work, so prosecution was unnecessary.

In addition to non-violent demonstrations, the cases of desertion were becoming more common. For the most part, however, US attorneys seemed hesitant to refer cases of desertion to the Federal Courts. At one point, six objectors deserted a CPS camp in May, and four months later, the Department of Justice suggested that the registrants were eligible for discharge, although they had continued in a desertion status. The Assistant Attorney General stated to the Director of Selective Service in a letter dated 10 September 1946, "Public policy does not demand the prosecution of these cases; consequently, no further action in these camps is contemplated by this department."

The degree or severity of the unrest in church sponsored CPS camps will probably never be known because the men were often protected by the sympathetic camp director who was a member of a Peace Church, and he reported to the Selective Service System. A problem assignee would be transferred from work on the federal project to an office job or to camp overhead. He would be out of view of the government employees and his resistance would never be reported.

CPS—THE END

Because of the protests and unrest, some of the Federal agencies operating the camps were preparing to discontinue the projects termed work of national importance.[21]

The public was critical of the government for its lack of control and lack of legal action against the conscientious objectors. The American Legion passed a resolution condemning the government and authorized its commander to bring the facts before the President of the United States.

Initially, the majority of the churches thought of themselves as providing the religious, social, and spiritual environment for their men while the government was responsible for the conscription and work.

Toward the end of the war, the Peace Churches were beginning to question the issue of conscription and the relation of the church and state in operating the CPS camps. Were the churches merely "serving as 'straw bosses' for forced labor as part of the army machine and were they running a part of the Selective Service System (conscription) as are the draft boards?" The three peace churches addressed this issue more intensely and more frequently as the war continued.[22]

The Quaker and Brethren camps experienced some resistance at an early stage because of the absolutist type objectors. They not only objected to war, but they objected to the whole psychology of conscription. The Mennonite Church had few problems because of its attitude of submission.

By 1945, the National Service Board for Religious Objectors (NSBRO) reported it was making fewer decisions and Selective Service was making more. Some church members felt this loss of authority in the camps caused the spirit of non-cooperation to grow, which increased more government control, which increased the spirit of non-cooperation. In addition, the types of work requested by the federal agencies were becoming less important. One year before the end of conscription, the American Friends Service Committee actually withdrew from CPS and turned its

21   Facts in this chapter are taken from Selective Service System. *Conscientious Objection: Special Monograph*. Vol 1. No. 11. Washington, DC: Government Printing Office, 1950. p. 229-251.

22   Hershberger, Guy Franklin. T*he Mennonite Church in the Second World War*. Scottdale, PA: Mennonite Publishing House, 1951. p. 270.

camps over to Selective Service. Most members of NSBRO felt that improvements were desirable in the CPS program and began a new written draft before the war had ended.

The Selective Service summary of the CPS experiment was that "scant attention was given to the conscientious objectors' welfare along such lines as pay, allowances, and allotments." They also felt a more effective procedure should be set up for identifying the maladjusted registrants and that regulations and laws should be changed to allow for prompt discipline in camps.

CHANGES IN SELECTIVE SERVICE REGISTRATION REQUIREMENTS AND DRAFT LAWS

The "Germfask" men, along with the various peace organizations, fought for recognition of the concept that man can be opposed to war on moral or ethical beliefs as well as religious beliefs. However, it wasn't until 1965, in the *United States v. Seeger* decision, that the Supreme Court broadened the definition of conscientious objection to include religious beliefs that are nontraditional and nontheistic in nature. In 1970 in Welsh v. *United States,* the Supreme Court officially defined ethical and moral beliefs as a basis for conscientious draft objection.

After World War II, in the 1950s, Selective Service renamed Civilian Public Service, "Alternative Service," and later it was called "Voluntary Service." From World War II through the Vietnam War, men classified IV-E were required to do work of national importance. They served for the same length of time as drafted men and received a stipend. They volunteered for various assignments and did humanitarian work throughout the world. Some still volunteered to be human guinea pigs for medical experiments.

American's anti-war sentiment during and following the Vietnam War resulted in Congress ending the draft in 1973. The United States converted to an All-Volunteer military and local draft boards were disbanded.

In 1980, legislation was passed to reinstate draft registration without authorizing induction, and to reinstate the local draft board. Few American citizens are aware that trained draft boards are in place and prepared to act. The boards are required to meet once a year, during which time a paid employee of Selective Service gives them updates on new legislation or pending legislation. Mock hearings are presented and discussed.

From 1980 to the present time, all male citizens between the ages of eighteen and twenty-six are required to register for the draft. Failure to register for the draft is a felony. All registrants could become eligible for training and service until the age of thirty-five.

PART II

THE RESEARCH CONTINUES, THE PROJECT COMPLETED

In 2005, with the aid of a computer, it was possible to find several former Germfask conscientious objectors. Dan Dingman and Nick Migliorino lived in Tampa, Florida and Arden Bode lived in California. It was agreed we would meet in Tampa at Dan's home. Marcus Rosenbaum, Senior Editor, Special Projects at National Public Radio, joined our group.

Marcus Rosenbaum interviewing Dan Dingman in the Dingman's backyard.

Author's photo

(Mr. Rosenbaum's interviews can be heard at http://www.npr.org/templates/story/story.php?storyId=4725447. The broadcast was titled "Recalling a U.S. Camp for WWII's Unwilling Draftees.")

DAN DINGMAN

Author Interview May 11

Dan: I believe I was the only CO to have been in a religious camp, all four Selective Service CPS camps, and federal prison. I wore a maroon crew cap during most of my CPS days. In every camp and prison that I was confined, I always spoke and acted as though I was an honored guest.

I had to go to prison to complete my mission. I wanted to go to prison. I went to prison by choice. Nobody should have to accept conscription. I turned down contracts because they were government-related for the military.

Jane: What did you think about Norman Nelson?

Dan: He was a strange one. He was completely baffled. He threatened us. He thought he'd scare us. Selective Service will get you! Almost nothing happened. After Jack Hood was tried and he found out only the federal courts had control of us, he was completely exasperated. He had no control. We didn't care. We simply didn't care what they did to us. It's impossible to control or scare people if they have no fear of the consequences. Nelson didn't want to call attention to us. I can understand the war was necessary, and I do not mean to demean the men who fought in it. Your interest, curiosity, after all these years vindicates our actions.

Jane: What was your life like after the war?

Dan: After returning home, I got permission from my parole officer, also one of my professors, a pacifist himself, to get married.

After we got married, we moved to California. It was difficult for a conscientious objector to find work. I interviewed for a position as a construction estimator by a man who reported directly to Walt Disney. He told me they did not have an opening in California but had plans to construct a Disney World in Florida, and he offered me the job. I told him I was a conscientious objector.

He said, "I didn't ask that question; can you do the job?"

I told him I could.

We packed our old car with our children and a few possessions. We drove to Orlando where I immediately began working for Disney. This was prior to public disclosure about the project. I was hired to calculate a total cost for construction. I told them it would be $400,000,000.00.

If you walk along Main Street, USA at Disney World, you will see my name on the camera shop window. It is under the awning and says, "Buena Vista Construction Co. My title there is *Reckoner.*

Jane: A Germfask women told me some men from your camp raped a girl in Newberry. She said a crowd was waiting for them when they went back the next weekend but the men escaped and there was never an investigation.

Dan: No, it didn't happen. There was an angry mob that attempted to do great bodily harm to some of our men, but it wasn't because of a rape. It was because we were conscientious objectors. Al Partridge took the brunt of the attack. It was a terrorizing situation.

A few days later the police came to camp and said if we were in town again, they'd be sure to be gone.

Occasionally on Saturday night, someone would come into camp and show us a movie. Some of the local children came to watch it with us. Other than that we had very little contact with the residents, with the exception of a work supervisor's family who lived across the street from the camp. Their young son enjoyed riding his bike through the camp and his parents didn't object to him being around us.

Jane: I was told one of your supervisors carried a gun and threatened to shoot you if you didn't work.

Dan: That is absolutely false. Never, in Germfask or any other camp were men threatened with guns. The government personnel did not carry guns and there were no guns in camps.

Dan passed away in 2013. During his entire life, his convictions never wavered. He stayed absolute in his opinions.

At Southern Florida University, he asked to speak at a veterans meeting to explain his objection to war and conscription. He was well-accepted by them, and from that meeting, a chapter of Veterans for Peace was organized on campus. He attended those meetings regularly. He was a Guardian Ad Litem volunteer, a voice for abused and neglected children in court, and he supported The Center on Conscience & War.

DAN DINGMAN MEMOIR: MY LIFE AS A CONSCIENTIOUS OBJECTOR (PACIFIST)

PART 1

PACIFIST BACKGROUND

"Gonna lay down my sword and shield,

Down by the riverside,

Down by the riverside,

Gonna lay down my sword and shield,

Down by the riverside,

Down by the riverside,

Ain't gonna study war no more!"

In our china cabinet is an ivory teething ring attached to a tiny silver bell, which is inscribed with the initials "E.L.D." and the date "Jan. 13, 1919." Eugene Lansing was the sixth of my eight brothers. However, he died in infancy long before I was born. Also, somewhere in my family documents is a Jersey City ballot with my father running for a local judgeship on the same Socialist party ticket with Eugene Debs for president. Debs ran for president four or five times, and while imprisoned as a pacifist, received over 900,000 votes in 1920. It is obvious it was he after whom Eugene Lansing was named.

And, on my mother's desk in the downstairs front hallway of our home at 7 Grove Street in Palmer, Massachusetts, was an electric lamp—the base of which was a World War I bombshell casing. On this casing was a metal band inscribed with the biblical quotation, "They shall beat their swords into plowshares, and their spears into pruning hooks: nation shall not lift up sword against nation, neither shall they learn war any more" (Isaiah 2:4).

It has also been family lore that my great-grandfather, I don't even know on which side, was twice imprisoned in the same location by both sides in the Civil War for refusing to take up arms. (A civil war—that's a real oxymoron!)

Anyhow, though in my youth I had more than one cap pistol and numerous popguns and rubber band guns and loved to play the Red Baron against my best friend Billy Brouillette's French airplane on our upside-down porch rocking chairs, I don't think I really was anything but a pacifist.

It was always apparent to me that both my parents were pacifists, though I don't recall any particular manifestations of it, and I'm afraid—as I think back at his letters to Congress and the newspapers—that my father was somewhat of an isolationist as well.

My parents were, I believe, affiliated with a Reformed Evangelical Lutheran church before moving, but in Palmer, they became members of, and active in, the Second Congregational Church. Like most of my brothers before me, I also did.

While many Protestant churches had their own denominational youth groups, Christian Endeavor encompassed many different churches, and it was in this group that I was most active. I met many friends through them, and always argued for the pacifist position at meetings and conferences—even though as the Second World War approached, more and more of the pastors began to hedge their positions.

I cannot for the life of me figure out why we as a family were returning home from Grandma's house in Jersey City on December 7, 1941, but I vividly remember that that's where we were when we heard President Roosevelt announce the Japanese attack on Pearl Harbor. It was a Sunday, and the following day, as senior class president, I was called on to lead the pledge of allegiance at a special high school assembly. I demurred and called on a classmate to take my place, as I did not wish to endorse what was certain to be a call to arms. This was acceptable to the school authorities, as my position had already been obvious to all.

On one occasion, I had flunked an essay on "Why We Should Buy War Bonds" when I wrote "Why We Should <u>Not</u> Buy War Bonds." When Phys-Ed became military training, I also declined and wound up doing cross-country running by myself for that period. On another later occasion, it worked to my advantage. As part of the wartime hysteria, groups of students volunteered to man nighttime observation posts in case of enemy air attacks. One day, police arrived and called some of my friends out of class for questioning. It seems that the students' tour of duty became so monotonous that they took to egg-throwing in a Home-Ec room and ended up doing considerable damage.

Despite the general wartime climate, I don't recall any overt reaction to my position, although it was sometimes a matter of discussion with friends who either could not agree or could not understand why I made such a big deal of it. In more than one case, I definitely felt that friends actually agreed with me but felt family pressure not to take a stand. Fortunately, I had no such problem.

Brothers Wes, Stan, Lester, and eventually Bob all received deferment for family, job, or in Bob's case, physical reasons. Brothers Paul and Raleigh, neither of whom ever saw combat service, accepted their draft calls, but fully supported brother Gerry's position and mine, as also did my younger sister, Bette, and both our parents. Gerry applied for and received a IV-E, conscientious objector (CO) classification, and was sent to Civilian Public Service (CPS) Camp #32, operated by the Quakers in West Campton, New Hampshire. I registered for the draft in April, 1942, when I turned eighteen. I had intended to ignore registration, but my mother thought I should. So I did. She did not want me to go to prison for refusing to register.

I graduated from high school in June, rode my bicycle to Maine in the summer, and entered American International College in Springfield (fifteen miles from home) in the fall. Paul and Raleigh were still there at that time. Like Gerry, I had applied for IV-E status when I registered, and I was eventually called up for a hearing. The chairman of the local board was a member of our church and well-aware of my position, so he had no problem in granting me that classification.

PART 2

CIVILIAN PUBLIC SERVICE CAMPS

It was on a Saturday night, and the moon was shining bright

When they passed the conscription bill

And for miles and miles away you could hear the people say

It was the president and his boys on Capitol Hill.

He said: "I hate war, and so does Eleanor,

But we won't be safe 'til everybody's dead!

— Camp song

I had finished my first year of college before I was assigned to "service" at the same camp as Gerry in the summer of 1943. The West Campton camp, #32, was a former CCC barracks and our project was run by the

Forest Service, but I can't describe what was being done since I was there such a short time. I do recall one job there, though. It was to heat the drab white margarine in a pan until it softened to the point I could mix in the right amount of orange coloring to try to make it palatable for serving in the mess hall in place of butter.

At Campton, Gerry edited the underground newsletter "Action." He immediately booked me into their barracks of rebels. Genial Jim (James Mullin), the camp administrator, informed me that I would get along fine if I hung out with the right crowd and followed the rules. This was my first acquaintance with the radical element of CPS, "The Lewis B. Hershey Elite Guard." Gerry was a member of the Guard and a night watchman so it was convenient for us to meet in the mess hall after hours where it was warm and we feasted on meager rations left unprotected. Anagrams and anecdotes relieved our boredom, and long midnight walks gave us a vague sense of freedom. One discussion centered on how we could conserve tin cans without contributing to the war effort. Some CPS men gave 200 percent cooperation (Mennonites), but the Elite Guard was known as 10 percenters—a name that stuck beyond #32.

From the first evening on, I was a 10 percenter. I was no longer alone. I knew now that others felt as I did, and I was determined not to promote the official legend of complete cooperation and participation in the program.

Upon admittance to camp, I refused to take the required smallpox, diphtheria, and diarrhea inoculations, so I was sent to Plymouth along with six other conscientious objectors to see a doctor. We rode in the back of a green canvas-colored truck. In Plymouth was a sign on the barber-shop window: "NO SKUNKS OR CONCHIES ALLOWED." It was not just in Plymouth but in other towns that we spent fruitless hours waiting for service in eating places or getting maintenance on camp vehicles. Occasionally, rocks or rotten eggs would be thrown at us (in Manistique and Germfask).

I arrived back at Campton without the inoculations. I associated with the wrong group and began my passive resistance techniques. I botched up every job, labeling paint cans to cleaning water tanks. I got my first RTW when a wrench fell out of the back of the pickup and we conscientious objectors said nothing. A fourteen-year-old kid was working beside us for $.85 per hour while we received nothing. It started to rain, so we went under cover. The boss said he had not told us it was raining, so we must keep working. He bawled us out every fifteen minutes, made notations in his little black book, and finally wrung the water from his hat and authorized the rest of the crew to come in from the rain. Genial Jim made every effort to erase the blemish. He pardoned us and then told us only the foreman was qualified to determine whether it was raining. (Looks like conscientious objectors were successful in controlling this situation.)

I was given a work assignment at a side camp fifty miles farther north of Gorham, New Hampshire, along with three other men around my age: Art Emery, Ralph Metivier, and Hugh Bustin. That was a very pleasant experience. Our supervisor was an elderly forest service employee who drove us to our work locations in an old pickup truck. We maintained the roadside of gravel roads in the White Mountains, learning to use and sharpen huge scythes to cut the roadside grass. We also cleared mountain trails and scenic outlooks. The most fun was climbing Mt. Washington and restocking the first aid stations on the ski trails. Even in late summer, there were shaded areas where considerable snow remained. The only hazard encountered was riding in the back of a pickup with a driver who chewed tobacco!

After a month or two, I was called back to main camp and asked whether I wanted to go to the new government-operated camp in Mancos, Colorado, which had just been opened by my brother Gerry, several other non-Quakers from West Campton, and men from other camps. **As before mentioned, draftees were actually expected to pay for their own keep in church camps, and Gerry and I had had difficulty persuading our father that we did not wish him to keep paying for us. Of course, this was the situation with most other conscientious objectors not from traditional peace churches**. That, plus the fact that in general we did not subscribe to the "200 percent" co-operation continually exhorted at that camp, made officials anxious to be rid of responsibility for us. When given a form on which to indicate whether I wanted to be in a church camp or a government camp, I wrote "neither" and strongly reiterated that position when interviewed, refusing to make the decision for them. Eventually, they made the decision by asking me whether I wanted to remain at West Compton. To this, I gave a negative answer and was then notified that **I was transferred to CPS camp #111 in Mancos. This camp was set up for men not easily handled in church camps. My brother Gerry and George Baird were sent there primarily because they wrote *Action,* a CPS newspaper that gave the outside world one of the first inklings**

there was not 100 percent satisfaction with the camps. The "Elite Guard" died with West Campton, but the 10 percenters go on forever.

Shortly thereafter, I received my government issued orders, travel and food vouchers, and a ride to the train station. I had a travel companion, Al Schmeelk—a Jehovah's Witness in the same situation. We had one bit of excitement traveling cross-country in a train with a large number of soldiers. One of a group of intoxicated soldiers came over to ask us how come we were not in uniform. When he brought the news back, an agitated discussion ensued, and a girl with the bunch convinced them they should throw us off the train. When the same fellow came back with that decision, Al invited him to go ahead and try. Al is big, and it seems the Jehovah's Witness are not necessarily pacifists, but will only not kill if it is at the Lord's direction. The soldier retreated for further advice, but fortunately, at that time a senior officer arrived on the scene and quelled the disturbance. There were, however, a lot of nasty remarks when we got off in Denver.

Waiting to transfer to Denver, we had a much more pleasant experience. With plenty of time to spare, we visited the state capitol building. Standing on an outside deck of the building overlooking the city, we asked a young woman what one of the other buildings was. Instead of a simple answer, Merle Audrey Hill offered to give us a walking tour of the area. First, of course, she had to get her mother's okay. So we waited in the governor's reception area while a clerk took the message in to where Mrs. Hill was in conference with the governor. That cleared, we proceed on a delightful tour of a broadcast studio and several other facilities where she was known. Naturally, I wrote her a thank you letter, and got a nice letter in return. Surprisingly, I also had a note from her mother, which she did not want Merle to know about. She wrote that Merle told her who we were and that she didn't raise her son to be a soldier either, but when his country called, it was his duty to serve. Still, she appreciated our integrity, and thought that it was better than Merle's boyfriend, whom, she said, didn't believe in anything, "So, please write her again, and if you don't write, you're wrong!"

From Denver, we took another train to Alamosa, where we transferred to the Denver and Rio Grande Western narrow gauge railroad across the Rockies to Durango, Colorado. That last was a very interesting and exciting trip through steep mountainous country where the rail barely clung to the edge of precipitous drops. Nearing the highest point, a locomotive was sent down to couple on and help pull the train up the mountain. The dining car was so narrow that the tables were staggered from side to side, with the waiters weaving their way between them. The car was illuminated by gas lanterns. And, happening to look down, I could see the railroad ties flash by as I flushed the toilet. In Durango, we boarded "The Cannonball Express," an ancient bus that brought us to Mancos, where we were met by a camp vehicle.

The Mancos camp was operated by the Bureau of Reclamation. The project was the construction of an off-river dam for the Mancos River to provide an irrigation reservoir. First, the dam would be built in a small valley, and then the river would be diverted to create the reservoir. (I believe that when completed, the outflow was then returned to the original bed further downstream.)

Here, for the first time, a government entity was fully responsible for the operation of the camp and the needs of the draftees. The Bureau of Reclamation directed the project, but Selective Service controlled the conscientious objectors. Chuck Thomas was the director and was, "as honest a man as Chuck Thomas ever saw." We were issued GI type clothing, though not uniforms, nor were we required to wear them. We were provided clothing, food, shelter, and a $5 a month allowance for personal items. Those who were assigned supervisory duties received an additional $2.50, but generally, those who got it put it into a fund for minor celebrations for the whole group. The food was, I suppose, typical of any men-in-a-camp mess hall, except that the cook enhanced—expanded—our chicken menu, especially the legs, with the abundant jackrabbits that he loved to hunt. Discipline was rather lax, as there was no effective mechanism for punishment short of cumbersome court action. Yes, there were all sort of rules that were generally obeyed for everyone's mutual benefit, but complete defiance could only be met by the threat of apprehension by civil authorities for violation of the draft itself.

Because the camp was a catch-all for non-traditional conscientious objectors, there was a wide variety of attitudes toward conscription, cooperation, pacifism, and conscientious objection itself. For the most part, we chose our own barracks and "birds of a feather" tended to "flock together." Thus, one barracks became "Kingdom Hall," home of most of the Jehovah's Witnesses. The Jehovah's Witnesses (JWs), while not exclusionary, did conduct their own service, and sadly seemed to seek activities involving other JWs. But they did often join in other group activities, and I made many good friends among them. I was surprised to learn that many were determined not to father children because the End Time was likely to be upon us in the near future. A number of them were very boisterous and even seemed belligerent at times. Foul language, at least in my opinion, was even more prevalent among them than the general population. One notable exception was Bob LeCompte, about my age, with whom I became good friends. He took considerable ribbing while we were part of a general gabfest for protesting someone's expletive by saying, "Don't say, 'Sh-t.' Say, 'Fiddle-dee-dee!'" I have since had several occasions to quote that admonition myself.

There were a good many peace church members at Mancos as well—for various reasons, including not being able to, or willing to, pay for the privilege of being in a church camp. They and others who might not have belonged to such a church, or any church, also tended to group together.

I, of course, chose my brother's barracks, which was made up of much of the original group that came from West Campton, and a number of others of similar interests. In our barracks were a couple of Theosophists, a Catholic, a Jew, an avowed non-religious Socialist-Labor party pacifist, and several other denominations. I also recall, from another barracks, a contingency of followers of Father Divine, who were accused at mealtime of taking more than their share of food while assuring everyone: "Father will provide."

So much depended on local draft boards in deciding whether or not a person was entitled to a IV-E classification. Some boards were lenient, others harsh—and often downright vindictive, allowing no exemptions. A few, who otherwise would have easily qualified as 4-F, physically or mentally exempt, were given IV-Es by their board instead because they had expressed their opposition to the war. Forest Leever and Walter C. came to Mancos from the federal penitentiary at Chillicothe, Ohio, where they had been sent for refusing induction after being denied CO status. All of us knew friends in the armed forces who had either been denied CO status, or had not applied for it because of family or other social pressures.

Gerry had driven his car to Mancos rather than coming by government voucher, so we had several opportunities to visit the many interesting places in the vicinity. We visited Mesa Verde National Park with its fascinating cliff dwellings. Another time we went to Shiprock, New Mexico, and unsuccessfully tried climbing that awesome butte, a feat I don't think anyone accomplished until thirty or forty years later. We did, however, succeed in climbing Mt. Hesperus, a peak well over 13,000 feet. We also were able to enjoy Thanksgiving dinner that year with the Fisherdicks at their ranch in Heperus. Cyrus Fisherdick was the brother of a family friend back in our hometown.

Closer to camp, on a walk one day, I discovered a pottery shard. I started digging and not only found many more pieces, but actually a whole human skull! I had hopes of trying to reconstruct the broken pottery. However, I learned that it was illegal to dig up or possess ancient Indian artifacts. They were dutifully turned over to the camp director for delivery to Mesa Verde authorities. I asked several times for a report on their disposal but never received one, a fact which made me believe the director, who was fascinated by such things, may never have turned them in. (I wrote Mesa Verde years later and received a reply that they could find no record of such an incident.)

The camp itself was at an elevation of 7,800 feet, and the air was clearer and purer than anywhere else I have ever been. Walking on a moonless night in the winter, we could actually see a vague shadow moving on the snow beneath us from the brightness of the stars above.

Several times, a group of us went into town for Sunday night dinner at the Mancos hotel. Reservations were required and the meal was served family style. The only choice was in your drink—coffee, tea, or water. But it was very pleasant and a nice change from the fare at camp.

I also remember an almost pleasant visit to the dentist there. Well, it was the least unpleasant dentist's visit I had ever had. His office was in his home and the drill was a foot treadle operated so there was no noisy motor sound and his control of the drill's speed and pressure was so good I never felt any pain.

I understood there were also a lot of negative feelings to having conscientious objectors in the area, although I never personally encountered them at that camp. A few of the men's wives had rented places in town to be near their husbands and they spoke of snubs they received. The local doctor refused to see the pregnant wife of one camper.

I early gained a reputation as a troublemaker at Mancos, and it was not altogether unearned. Like many others in this diverse group, in addition to my religious objections to war and killing, I was, and am, totally opposed to the conscription system and had no intention of cooperating with it.

This meant that I would, at the most, do only what was necessary to avoid being prosecuted. And, knowing that camp officials had very little mechanism for penalizing minor infractions, I performed most assignments in a pretty unsatisfactory manner—from their point of view. Gerry and I differed somewhat on this point. He and others chose rather to challenge the system on technical grounds—such as the fact that camps were actually under military control contrary to law and that we were being forced to work without pay. Neither, of course, affected any change in policy.

The first incident of wage payment protest occurred when one of the campers, Jim, asked every day what the wages were. When told he would not be paid, he went back to the barracks and Refused to Work (RTW). After a few weeks, he was arrested and prosecuted and spent one-and-a-half years in federal prison. I believe if the men would have organized behind Jim at this time, they may have made a case for no pay from the court system. (Of course, the churches did not support the opinions of the anti-conscription protesters.)

In January or February of 1944, a number of us (presumably including those who had received similar evaluations) got transfer orders to the second government operated camp, CPS Camp #128 at La Pine, Oregon. A dozen or more of us made that trip by train with government travel and food vouchers. It included a half-day stopover in San Francisco, where I got my first taste of California.

The La Pine camp was located on the Deschutes River near Bend, Oregon. As I recall it, the Wickiup Dam had already been completed, and our project was clearing of a forest on land, which would be flooded as the water rose. This was also a Bureau of Reclamation project. I remember being fascinated by the pieces of volcanic rock that floated to the surface when thrown in the water because of the air pockets in them. Some of the trees to be removed were two or three feet in diameter. After we properly notched them with double-bladed axes, we sawed them off a foot or two above ground level and sawed them with two-man hand saws. We sometimes managed to line two trees up in a row so the first knocked the second down as it fell. I still have a faint scar on my left knee where a saw tooth nicked me when we tried to pull it out as one tree twisted and almost hit Romeo Frechette and me as it fell. Still, the work was so interesting and exciting that I almost enjoyed it.

Rather than refusing an assignment, I would plead ignorance and wait for directions on how to accomplish the task. Then I would try to construe the instructions in the most impractical way possible. Told to trim the branches on a tree so it could be cut down, I needed to know what tool to use, where one could be found, which branch to cut first, how close to the trunk to cut it off, etc. After it was thoroughly explained and demonstrated to me, the foreman observed my first few cuts and went on his way. I was over twenty feet up in the tree when he came back a few hours later and clarified the point that trimming was only required for a few feet off the ground. The purpose of such actions on my part was to protest the illegality of the unpaid Civilian Public Service camp program in particular, and the entire conscription system in general. (Well, I must admit that I also took a great bit of enjoyment in it at the time, treating it as a great game, and being pleased at the support and encouragement I got from other similarly minded campers!)

I also worked on a survey crew for several months and then was assigned to go into man-dug test hole pits to determine the soil types. We had to figure out when blasting would be done and get out of the way. Because of its danger, I refused to go and got RTW. I was then put to work out of the way (side camp) cutting poles for rock-crushers. The crew took turns as lookout, made a campfire, and read most of the day.

Next, I was assigned to work in the craft shop where I carefully nailed three lockers into the forms. I was assigned to restacking lumber, nailing each board to the next one; next, three of us were assigned to painting with two brushes. We worked for two weeks until the 200 percenters protested and finished the job in forty-eight hours. After this, I developed a regular 99.4 degree morning temperature and went permanently SQ and "<u>never did another lick of loafing on projects at Mancos</u>."

Camp officials came up with the bright idea of having problem campers reclassified as 4-F to get them out of the way. A number of us were sent to Salem to be interviewed by psychiatrists. This was the correct thing because several men who should never have been conscripted in the first place received their release. But I am sure the administration was disappointed when, in my case, the report they got was: "this nineteen year Massachusetts malcontent is not ill from a neuro-psychiatric point of view, but has joined with a group of other malcontents to disrupt the camp."

I, like many others, was becoming increasingly aware that by accepting our own personal exemptions from military service, we were actually facilitating the smooth operation of the system, and thus were not effectively protesting the conscription of others who could not convince their draft boards of their right (actually, everyone's right) to refuse to kill. Over time, many in church camps as well as government camps had become absolutists on this point, made a statement of their position, and walked out of camp to defy the system.

We could only speculate on the reasons why, but in May, most of the same group were transferred again, this time off to CPS Camp #135 in Germfask—in Michigan's Upper Peninsula. The camp had just been opened—once again by brother Gerry and a bunch of his group from Mancos. It appeared that this was supposed to be the Alcatraz of CPS camps, where all the radicals, misfits, malcontents, and troublemakers could be gathered out of everyone's way. That was not to be.

The Upper Peninsula of Michigan was, and I guess still is, sparsely settled, and Germfask was a very small community on the edge of the Seney National Wildlife Refuge. Blaney Park, a few miles south of the camp, claimed to be the birthplace of Paul Bunyan, and had a huge statue of him by the roadside. It made sense because the area had been victimized by lumbermen who years ago had stripped much of the peninsula of its forests.

(Geographic sidelight: the nearby Manistique River was known as the river that flowed in both directions. In the spring, it flowed north, bringing melting snow into Manistique Lake. Because the land was practically flat, in the summer the overfilled lake flowed back south, carrying the logs down into Lake Michigan.)

Our camp was practically in Germfask, the name of which I learned was an anagram of the initials of the first eight settlers. Because our occasional Saturday night movies were the only entertainment around, local youth often joined us for the show. Many of us struck up acquaintances with some of them who did not seem to have any qualms about associating with us conchies. Other locals were not as happy about our presence. In one instance, the parishioner who fired up the furnace for Sunday services at the Catholic mission refused to heat the place as long as anyone from the camp attended.

None of the camps I was in was large enough to have any medical facility larger than a first aid room, usually staffed by either a civilian nurse or an assignee. When someone's claim of illness was either suspect or serious, the procedure would be to send him to a local practitioner or hospital. At Germfask, however, the destination for the ill was a POW camp for captured German soldiers, located some distance away. Those who made the trip reported that the facilities there were better than ours—and they, of course, could not be required to work.

Our assignment at Germfask was to replace the missing staff of the Fish and Wildlife Service in maintaining the wildlife refuge. As usual, I was not a star co-operator and never got a proper view of the overall scope of the project. I do recall a rather pleasant spell where I spent a lot of time reading books while dutifully opening and shutting a pasture gate for the occasional vehicle that had business inside. Another time I was on a wire fence mending crew. However, I had difficulty comprehending the superintendent's detailed instruction on how to use a hammer and staples. Since he failed to clarify the final desired result, I had almost a hundred staples in that post before he redirected my efforts. Harvey Saunders was a really nice fellow, though, and he seemed to understand the motive of such resistance, even though he could not condone it. Thereafter, it seemed that whatever the purported purpose was, my actual assignment basically resulted in my simply spending the days out of his way in the wide open spaces of the refuge.

As a wildlife refuge, the area abounded in both birds and animals, including deer and bears. Once I frightened some resting deer by almost stumbling over them while jogging through the underbrush. Another time, walking with Frank Hatfield, he stepped into a clump of bushes to see what was moving about in there; suddenly, he came charging back out toward me, while a frightened bear took off in the other direction! But the most memorable sight was on a walk one brightly moonlit evening when we had the rare privilege of seeing deer dancing. Across the meadow from the road, several deer were lined up in a row like an audience. First one deer and then another would step out, prance around, then step back and watch the next one! It was a sight I will never forget.

In June or July of that year, I received a letter from a friend in which she mentioned that she was going to visit relatives in a small town near Muncie, Indiana, that summer, and I decided to visit her there. Whatever leave time I might have accumulated over the past year had either been used or revoked for various infractions of camp rules. So I used a weekend pass instead, altering the end date to cover the period I expected to be gone, and went on my way. I can't remember details of the trip, but it was at least 400 or 500 miles and must have taken more than one day hitch-hiking. At almost the end of the trip, I was stopped by a highway patrol-man who wanted some identification. In those days, men my age not in uniform were often under suspicion, but it may also be that he was alerted by my talk with my most recent driver. In any case, although dubious, he accepted my credentials and story and I completed my trip. Once there, I dropped a note to the highway patrol, to the attention of the badge number I had noted. I explained that the whole authorization was phony, but that having come so far, I wanted to get to my destination, which I then listed for him. I said I would be there three days and then be heading back the same way I came. Which is what happened, without further incident—either on the trip or when I arrived back at camp. Thereafter, Saunders referred to anyone's unexcused absence as a "Danny Dingman" furlough.

One morning in early March of 1945, Gerry told me he had had a "visit" from "Mom" during the night. She was standing at the side of his bunk and told him she was dying, and that she was worried about brother Raleigh, who was in the army in Hawaii. We were shortly called to the office for a telegram confirming that she had died during the night. Fortunately, no ill had befallen Raleigh, although he was the only one who was unable to at-tend Mom's funeral. Gerry and I made the trip home by bus and train. This was before the bridge was built across the Mackinac Straits to the Lower Peninsula, and it was awesome to watch the icebreaker churning up the ice ahead of the ferry and the ice closing in again behind us. Several hundred yards away cars were driving across on the ice. We had a several hours layover in Albany, so we took in a movie. *Roxie Hart* was a very popular film, but I remember nothing about it, except that it was a funny feeling—taking time to see a movie on the way to my mother's funeral.

Sometimes, not too frequently, I and one or two others went to church in Manistique, about twenty-three miles to the southwest on Lake Michigan, but I can't remember how I (we) got there. I think the camp provided a covered truck for those who wanted to go to town on Sunday; I know one often took men north to the town of Newberry on Saturday evenings for the movies—and bars. On Sunday, two of us were embarrassed by a minister who had asked everybody to bow their heads and then called on anyone who was ready to be saved to raise his hand. Next, he asked everyone to pray for two young men who had seen the light. We got a lot of undeserved greetings when we left from people who thought he must have been referring to us.

More fun was the time we arrived to find the church packed, though we did manage to squeeze into the balcony. It turned out that the occasion was the return of a hometown girl, Maude Oberg, who had gone off to Chicago years ago and become the moll of Al Capone or one of his cronies. She had repented of her ways and was back to warn youngsters of the pitfalls of the big city. It seemed, though, that most of the crowd was more interested in hearing about her sins than her repentance. To me, it appeared that her story as she told it was more likely to recruit girls than to deter them.

The Saturday night Newberry trip was looked forward to by many, partly because liquor was not permitted in camp. It was also just a chance to get away from the camp and maybe to see a more recent movie or get something other than the camp fare to eat. I went infrequently, being neither a drinker nor a gourmet. But it was on one of those trips, when the weather was cold, that I smoked my first cigar—never really enjoying it, but happy to be part of the group. And it was on another one of those trips that I had my first alcoholic drink. It started out as a plain Coke, but we were having a problem with one of the fellows who wanted to keep sipping and talking when the rest of us thought we should leave. Sitting next to him, I managed to get quite a bit of his last two drinks into my last two Cokes. It wasn't bad at all and I suffered no ill effect. But it did the trick; we got him on the truck and back to camp. And I went back to soft drinks for many years.

I wasn't along on the BIG trip—the one that brought about all the furor and scandalous stories. It was just another one of those Saturday night Newberry trips at first, and I can't remember just what happened after that. Suffice to say, some of our boys had undoubtedly had too much to drink and took offense at the usual dirty digs we conchies regularly got almost anywhere we went. One thing led to another and some scuffles ensued. The local police broke it up before anyone was seriously injured; all of the fellows were herded back onto the truck, and the night on the town was over. But not the repercussions! First the Newberry paper reported on the event, and the fact that slackers were freeloading off the government and enjoying themselves while "our boys" were risking their lives overseas. Then the Chicago papers picked up the story, elaborated on it, and sent reporters up to see just how bad the situation was. Of course, camp director Norman V. Nelson was only too happy to explain that he really had no control over us, lacking an effective means of discipline. Then they visited the bohemian barracks that we actually took great pride in keeping as un-military looking as possible. And, naturally, they interviewed several of the most dissatisfied men, who explained why we saw no reason to co-operate with such an unjust system. The *Chicago Tribune* used its special red front page headline to proclaim: "CONSCIENTIOUS OBJECTOR CAMP IN OPEN REVOLT." Even *Time* magazine reported on the lack of discipline and general unruliness in the camp. The Escanaba, Michigan (about ninety miles southwest on the shore of Lake Michigan) paper was a little more objective, and ran a several-page report, including interviews with and photographs of many men in the actual camp setting. The cover-age in various papers lasted for some time. Mr. Voelker, a member of the camp administration, resigned in sympathy with us, in protest of the conditions conscientious objectors were subjected to in camps.

A direct result of this commotion was a virtual camp lockdown, with no leaves or passes for anyone. Unfortunately, this was close to Easter, and Dick Lazarus, Bent Andresen, and I were determined to go to Easter church services in Manistique. We left camp before sunup to walk the eight miles to the main highway to catch the morning Greyhound to Manistique, being deliberate in buying round-trip tickets to prove we were only going to church. We didn't think we were being particularly conspicuous. After church, we walked to the Eat Shop for a meal. A state policeman came in. He was a kind man, and after asking to see our papers, which we didn't have, he went to the counter and drank a cup of coffee while we finished eating. He escorted us to his car to his headquarters for more questioning. He phoned camp for verification that we were indeed AWOL, despite our obvious intention to return after church.

Director Nelson told them we were not to be returned to camp but de-tained for prosecution. With that, we were taken to the Manistique jail. It was really not a bad place, except for the old magazines and sticky play-ing cards. The jail was on the second floor of an older frame building, and fortunately, we had the place to ourselves. The jailer was friendly and so-ciable, and the food home-cooked by his wife, was good. Monday morn-ing, looking out the barred window, we could see the school bus unload-ing Germfask students. Recognizing Dotty Berry as one of the kids who came to our camp movies, I called to her. She was surprised, of course, but promised to tell my brother Gerry what had happened to us since we knew the director would never have bothered to. Gerry had had consider-able legal training, and he and two lawyers in the camp immediately got the word out to our families and began a letter-writing campaign on our behalf. Dick's mother was a lawyer of some influence in Washington, I believe, and among them, they managed to start some wheels in motion.

Meanwhile, we were transferred across the peninsula to the county jail in Marquette, Michigan, on the shore of Lake Superior, to await arraignment in federal court on charge of violation of the Selective Service Act by desertion from camp. This was certainly a more modern and impressive facility although we were once more alone. The jail keeper, again a very pleasant person, apologized for the fact that as federal prisoners, he had to segregate us on the third floor. This was because the third floor had tempered steel bars on the windows. A few years earlier, he said, two federal prisoners on the first floor had obtained a hacksaw and cut through the window bars on their cell. On two consecutive nights, they had slipped out, stole cigarettes, candy, and presumably other items to be used in an escape, and returned and hid them in their cell. Their selfishness did them in, however, as another inmate squealed when they refused to share with him, and they were caught on the third night as they prepared to leave for good. He also enjoyed telling us other stories. Like how the local sheriff often let solid local citizens jailed for drunkenness or the like go home after dark if they returned before daybreak. Or how the sheriff "furloughed" some prisoners to his ranch to work for him in return for the greater freedom it offered them. He also would check to see whether we wanted him to purchase anything for us on his trips uptown. Thus, at least we had clean playing cards and current reading material to while away the time. I celebrated my twenty-first birthday there, and on April 12, 1945, we got the news that President Roosevelt had died.

A few day later, the jail keeper walked us up to the courthouse for our arraignment. On the way, we passed a tobacco store, and he kindly waited while Bent went in for some pipe tobacco. The arraignment proceeding was a fairly simple affair. We were fingerprinted and advised what the charge against us was, and we each entered our plea of not guilty. The magistrate then released us on our own recognizance without bail pending trial. Funny, I can't remember at all how we traveled away from there. I think we were transported back to camp on the assumption that that was where we belonged. We certainly didn't see it that way. We had been freed on our own recognizance, and to us that meant "free"! So we each went home.

Thanks to Gerry and Frieda Lazarus and many others, a lot of sentiment had been generated for three men who were being prosecuted just for going to church on Easter Sunday. Selective Service apparently didn't want to push the case under those circumstances, so they sought a way out. Eventually, it was agreed that if we would return to camp, they wouldn't press charges. I, for one, really preferred to stay out and face the charge. But others argued that we had already made our point and it would be better to close the case. So back to camp we went—after an interesting adventure and a nice vacation. I did follow up with a letter demanding my fingerprint card back since there was no conviction—and I got it!

At Mancos and La Pine, there was always talk of walking out of camp as a more emphatic way of protesting conscription and war, rather than just accepting our own exemptions and remaining quiet. At Germfask, every month or so, another one or two men would make the decision to walk out, write a statement, and leave. Others felt it would be more effective if we had a mass walkout, capitalizing on the widespread notoriety the camp already had, to get the maximum publicity for our position. I tried hard to organize such an event at Germfask, but it always seemed that those tentatively in agreement felt that it would need just a few more than whatever number were signed up to make it truly effective. **On May 7, Germany surrendered and with possible release in sight within the foreseeable future, many—especially those who had been in the longest or whose families had suffered the most financially—dropped consideration of anything that would interfere with getting out legally.**

Meanwhile, maybe at the request of Fish and Wildlife and after all the negative publicity, just thirteen months after it had opened, Camp Germfask was closed and the remaining men were transferred to CPS Camp 148, Minersville, California, with Bliss Haynes, as camp director. It was opened just to accommodate our group, and a few misfits from other camps. Gerry and the boys continued to write, publish, and distribute *The Germfask Newspaper*. Although Minersville was definitely our mailing address, it has no ZIP number now and does not appear on AAA's California road map, nor in the Rand McNally atlas. It was, as I recall, not far from Weaversville, which *is* still on the map, about fifty miles northwest of Redding and in the Shasta-Trinity National Forest. This was a Forest Service location, and the primary objective was assisting in fighting forest fires—a clever assignment to give us, since most of us were not about to make an issue of putting out a fire. We were given training in fighting fire with axes, hoe, and shovels, as well as with water backpacks.

My most exciting adventure there was when a group of eight of us were assigned to a forest service man and an Indian guide and sent to extinguish a blaze in a very remote area. After riding as far as the truck could go, we were given two days' food ration, our tools and backpacks, and sent on our way. The first morning after a day's hike, the forester advised us that the guide not only had not found the fire, but had deserted the expedition during the night! The radio communication with base was not too good, but we continued on in what appeared to be the right direction. By late afternoon, hot and tired like the rest of us, he gave up, and we bedded down for the night's rest before trying to find our way home—or at least out of the forest. With no good clues as to where we were, we ditched all our gear (rations were already gone) and followed the policy of heading down until we found a stream, and following the stream to civilization. It was the right plan, although we almost lost the lead man when he suddenly came upon a steep cliff. Just finding a way down took over an hour, but we did find a stream at the bottom. Much of the way we had to walk in the water, so we took off soggy pants, but left heavy boots on. We finally came to a simple bridge on a dirt road. Not knowing which way to head, the forester called a break for a much needed rest. And we lucked out! In a couple of hours, a car came by and agreed to give him a ride to the nearest phone. Before nightfall, a forestry truck picked us up and the adventure was over. They never heard from the guide again, but we did learn that the fire had been put out by a bunch of Boy Scouts on a camping trip! That was also about the end of my forest-fighting experience. I did actually apply for a smoke-jumping detachment, but that was considered a choice assignment so I didn't get much consideration.

Besides, it was increasingly evident that the war would not last much longer. To most, as I mentioned, this was looked forward to as offering the possibility of release. Others were concerned that the war would end without their having made a sufficient testimony, to use a favorite Quaker term, "to their opposition to conscription." Gerry and I often discussed this issue, and while he was older and more conservative, he also understood my position. He had a business to get back to, while I was not yet established and felt very strongly about my need to take a stand. I felt then—and still do—that I would regret it if I always had to say that I accepted the privilege of not having to fight, when it should have been a right of every person. I wanted to go to prison to protest. So I said goodbye to Gerry and other friends and notified Director Haynes of my decision and walked out of camp and down the road.

PART 3

Between Gerry and me, I know I had a few dollars with me when I left camp. I did not, however, have a strategic plan in mind on how I was to get to Los Angeles, 600 miles to the south. I only knew that **in Los Angeles there was a safe haven for conscientious objectors known as Pacifica Center, or something like that, where I could stay while I got myself organized.** That was my destination, and Gerry was arranging to have our father send some money to me at that address. But first I had to get there.

I guess a lot of walking and a few rides got me to Redding, which I remember as a very beautiful city, perhaps because it was the first California community outside of San Francisco that I had really been in. From there it's about 150 miles to Sacramento, and I was there by nightfall. I got something to eat and slept on a park bench. Slept, that is, until a policeman wakened me by rapping on the soles of my shoes—a very effective wake-up method. Got through the night somehow and easily got a job (and a meal) washing dishes in a restaurant in the morning. But the place was sloppy and the rats in the basement where the supplies were kept were so intimidating that I quit by noon without getting any pay. I took a city bus to the edge of town and stopped in Sydenstricker's Drugstore for a piece of pie. I was so taken by the clerk that I spent some time talking and getting refills on a glass of water, and I obviously still haven't forgotten Rosalita Vasques.

It must have taken two days to cover the 450 miles to Los Angeles (this was way long before the interstate highway system). I don't remember where or how I spent the night—probably just walking the highway and thumbing rides. What I do remember is the fiercely hot weather around Fresno and Visalia, where I stood in the shade of a power pole while I hitchhiked. A kindly young Mennonite farmer picked me up and offered me a job helping him load hay where he was going. I tried, after he showed me the technique of grabbing the bale with a hook and tossing it onto the truck, but I was so hot and weak I couldn't do it. After he finished doing the job himself, he gave me a sandwich, drove me back to the highway, and gave me two dollars. A few rides later, three very cheerful black fellows offered me a ride the rest of the way to Los Angeles if I would help with the gasoline costs. There went the two dollars! Late in the afternoon, they declared mealtime and stopped in a shady place. We all had to get out so they could remove the backseat to retrieve a watermelon. In Los Angeles, they let me out somewhere we all thought must be close to my destination. Again, I don't recall how it happened, but by evening, I was at Pacifica, among new friends, and with a place to eat and sleep!

Los Angeles! What an exciting place for me to be. And what a different experience for me. Twenty-one years old, I had never really lived by myself before, except on a bicycle or hitch-hiking trip of some kind. Now, in a city, I had to find a job and a place to live. Both turned out to be quite easy. When the money from home arrived—enough, but not all that much, I found a room to rent, and checked the Help Wanted ads. My first interview was a success. I was hired by a rather seedy-looking man to set type in his rather seedy-looking Multigraph shop in a rather seedy-looking part of downtown. But it was my first job! (Except, of course, when I lived at home and worked for my father or as a dishwasher after school at a dairy store.)

My first weekend I went to Riverside to see a friend from camp. Jack Hood was one of the basically 4-F persons whom Gerry and his lawyer pals in camp had helped to get the right paperwork to get released. He and his folks were very cordial, and showed me what a great city Riverside was. We went to Mount Roubideaux and saw the view from there, and we also visited the great-grandparent of all navel oranges in this country—grown from a cutting from the original South American navel tree. That visit was really the inspiration for heading first to Riverside when we moved to California in 1952. One weekend, I went to Burbank to see where the Disney studios were. I had thought of trying to get a job there, but I never went through with it.

In Los Angeles, I was amazed by all the juice bars, which seemed to be quite the fad. Orange Julius, of course, but spinach and carrot and cauliflower juices? And then there were the two Clifton's Cafeterias, each with its own water fountains, waterfalls, and exotic settings. But their most unusual feature was that the signs all said you could pay what you could afford, or nothing, for your meal! The informality of the place meant you shared your table with anyone who came along and wanted to sit down. I met quite a nice young man there—I thought. We had a pleasant mealtime conversation, and he insisted on paying my bill. After which he gave me a ride home. But when he invited me to a movie, which I declined, and then suggested he come up to my room, I very firmly refused and said goodbye and shut the door. Live and learn!

Other memorable L.A. doings included: Going to church to hear Norman Vincent Peale preach; going by the Church of the Foursquare Gospel, founded by Aimee Semple McPherson; riding the original Angel's Flight up the hillside in downtown L.A.; buying my first suit at Bullocks on Wilshire Avenue; and seeing the famous Brown Derby Restaurant, and especially Earl Carroll's (whoever he was) Dinner Theater, where the single word "theater" consecutively flashes out "EAT," "AT," "THE," "THE-ATER," (or was it "theatre"?—either way, it seemed pretty neat to me). In those days, you could buy a weekly pass for both the yellow and green trolley (I forget its name) and the Big Red that took you out to many of the outlying areas, all for a very affordable price.

On August 14, after two horrendous atomic bombings, Japan surrendered, although it has been reported that they may have been seeking to negotiate a surrender a few weeks earlier. I joined the masses crowding Broadway and Seventh Streets, and I guess, everywhere else. It was the loudest and most boisterous celebration I have ever seen. Part of my celebration was spotting a second-story window with ACE Letter Shop printed on it. I went there the next day, got hired, and started work the following day, after letting the previous boss know I had a much better-paying job.

Ace Letter Shop was, in my opinion, a class act. The owner, George McNitt, and his wife worked there along with his three girls: Sally, Bonnie, and one whose name I can't remember. Before photocopiers and computers, Multigraph machines were the only economic way to mass-produce letters that actually looked like they were individually typed. The only difference between these machines and the Multigraph my father had, which I was very familiar with and had used for years, was that they were electric rather than hand-operated. (I still have our 1924 model in running condition.)

Ace Multigraph typed individual salutations, hand-signed, folded, and stuffed thousands of letters into envelopes; addressed, sealed, stamped, and mailed them for dozens of clients every week. My job was to help with any or all of these tasks, except the typing, plus occasionally running errands or making deliveries in the immediate area on orders that did not include mailing. Everyone was very helpful in getting me into the swing of things. They were all aware of my status, had no problem with it, and were happy to have extra help at a time when manpower was scarce.

One evening, my father called to let me know the FBI was looking for me. He said he'd had a phone call from the local chief of police, Tim

Crimmins, who said two agents had come asking him whether he could help them find me. He told them, "Sure, I'll just call Charlie Dingman and ask him." He did and my father gave them my address as Tim knew he would and I certainly wanted him to. The next day, I called the U.S. marshal's office and asked whether they had a warrant for my arrest. They did not, but I gave them my phone numbers at home and at Ace. They said they would call me if they heard anything. A week or two later, they called and said they had received the warrant, and would I come down so they could serve it, but since I was working, Saturday would be okay. I asked and was told the bail would be $1,500.00. Through a program already in place at Pacifica Center, a local engineer, Charles MacIntosh, whom I had never met, came down Saturday as soon as I called him from the courthouse and posted my bail!

It was then back to work, business as usual, until sometime later when a court date was set. Because the "offense" occurred in Northern California, the trial was to be in Sacramento. I was given the option of being transported by the government as a prisoner or having my bond released and traveling at my own expense on a personal guarantee of appearance in Sacramento. Naturally, I chose the latter, and Gerry came down from Minersville to travel with me, keep me company, and discuss strategy.

PART 4

"California has its charms, cities, town and spacious farms

Lovely maiden to allure you.

But, Oh Palmer! I assure you,

Prison bars are instrumental in keeping in Sacramento!"

— Anonymous

Now, I'm rather hazy about the correct sequence of events at that time, but I do recall a meeting with the prosecuting attorneys at which they urged me to plead guilty. A guilty plea might result in a lesser sentence, they said, but they immediately backtracked when I asked whether that was legal. And then they said that even if I won the first time, they could continue to charge me day after day for every succeeding day that I was AWOL until they got a jury that found me guilty.

I think it was on the first day of the trial, after I had come up in an elevator with a number of other prisoners and been placed in a holding area, that I was taken out of the "cage" by a bailiff for processing just before entering the courtroom for trial. Anyhow, he was then called out of the room for the moment. Immediately, my half-dozen fellow prisoners called to me to let them out! And it was a temptation. I mean, we were really all on the same (wrong) side of the law; they were my buddies, at least for the moment! But good sense prevailed, despite some rather mean words from them, and fortunately, the opportunity was very short-lived. That same day shortly after my trial, one of them did make a break for it. A former para-trooper, he slipped his guard on the way to the courtroom and jumped out a third-story window onto an adjacent one-story roof. Without his combat boots, the leap was too much and he fractured both ankles!

I, on the other hand, walked meekly into the courtroom for my trial. It was very cut-and-dried. I defended myself and admitted leaving the camp, but claimed I had been held illegally. The Fourteenth Amendment stipulates that neither slavery nor involuntary servitude shall exist, except as punishment for a crime of which one has been duly convicted. Since we received no compensation, it was obvious this constituted involuntary servitude and thus the law as administered was patently unconstitutional. But the judge quite improperly, I thought, told the jury they could not pass on the constitutionality of the law, only whether or not I left camp without permission. (Not that I or any other walk-out ever expected anything else.) And then this judge, who earlier the same day had levied two-year sentences on two walk-outs from other camps who entered guilty pleas, sentenced me to three years in federal prison! Gerry immediately filed the notice of appeal for me, and then he headed back to Minersville. I'll never know how much time and effort he and others spent on those appeals, but I am aware that all financially able family members sunk a good deal of money into them. There was an appeal to the Circuit Court, and then one to the Supreme Court, but both refused to hear challenges to the law and to General Hershey and Colonel Kosch's control of a system required by law to be under civilian direction.

I, meanwhile, was returned to the Sacramento County Jail. I spent the next few weeks there, wondering when I would be transferred to federal prison. It was not completely uneventful, though. I had as a cellmate, Toby Vasquez, who said he was related to Rosalita, previously mentioned. Toby also claimed he was tricked into signing a bad check for a friend whose writing hand was in a cast, and that's why he wound up in jail for a federal crime. So I never felt too sure about anything he told me. We were, however, about the same age and got along well together. One game we played was trying to get a match out of one of those tiny boxes of cigarette matches and strike it—using only our toes. And before I left the place, I managed to do it! Cigarettes—which I never smoked—were jailhouse issue, and we could trade them for other commissary items. I also was fortunate enough to have a few visitors while there. One was a local Congregational minister who thoughtfully brought fruit both times he came. That was my first experience with California avocados, and spread on bread from our morning meal, they made a great snack. Bread and oatmeal was the morning fare and the only meal until dinner. One time, with the help of an empty coffee can for a stove, we made ourselves some apple/pear sauce, also good on bread. Of course, fire was forbidden so we had to douse the flame in the toilet when the guard tried to find out where the smoke was coming from. A surprise visitor was Bonnie Wagner from the Ace Letter shop who persuaded her boyfriend to drive all the way up from Los Angeles just to pay me a visit!

After a few weeks in the Sacramento jail, I inquired as to why I was not being moved on to the federal prison, as had been the others convicted and sentenced the same day I had been. "Oh," I was told, "you appealed so you're automatically held here pending resolution of the case unless you request transfer to the prison." Moreover, it turns out my sentence would not even start until I reached prison! Naturally, on learning this, I requested, and the next day, I was on my way to McNeil.

Strange, but traveling on the train in a prison car felt more embarrassing to me than almost any other indignities I have endured or brought on myself. I mean, marching through the station two by two, handcuffed in pairs, with guards on either side. Everybody staring at you and wondering what sort of heinous crime you had committed. We really weren't being treated badly; it was just the idea of it. Anyhow, after a long trip, we arrived at Steilacoom, Washington, (amazing but just as I am typing this, it occurs to me how much that sounds like "steal a comb"!) and were transferred to the prison ferry and on to McNeil Island Federal Penitentiary.

Like, I suppose, at most federal penitentiaries, there were at least two types of facilities—in this case, the "big house" and the prison farm. The prison superintendent or warden was P.J. Squires, and the assistant for the "farm" was Stevens. At the time, I believe McNeil was considered one of the tougher prisons. Chillicothe, Ohio, was reputed to have more mental cases, and Danbury, Connecticut, was considered the country club of the system where high profile, white crime politico conscientious objectors and the like were sent and had private quarters with telephones, etc. Other facilities I know nothing about. McNeil Island is a big place. In addition to the several heavily secured and guarded main buildings, there was the large, barbed wire enclosed prison camp where minimum security prisoners lived in barracks. Beyond that were barns, chicken houses, orchards, and vegetable gardens, and a cannery. I learned that the federal prison facilities produced items that were distributed to other federal prisons and McNeil's farms produced food. I heard Chillicothe manufactured prison clothing, but I don't recall what others may have provided. Prison personnel and their families lived in a small community on the island and their children rode the ferry to school on the mainland. It was wistful to see them joking and playing as they awaited the bus to the ferry. One day on a work assignment in a field near the edge of the prison property, we were amused to see a housewife leaving her apartment, locking the door, and carefully putting the key up over the door.

When we arrived on the island, we were classified. The presumably more dangerous types, still in chains, were going directly to the "big house," and we less intimidating ones were being immediately lined up for processing, starting with shots. I explained that I had never been vaccinated and didn't choose to be now. Naturally, they said I didn't have a choice, and I had to agree, but I advised that if it were to be done, it would have to be done forcibly. There was some blustering and conferencing and then—surprise! I was passed along to the next interrogation without the shot! After being asked all kinds of questions, I was given a number, "FPC 1968" (the letters standing for Federal Prison Camp), my prison garb, a receipt for whatever personal belongings I had, paperwork telling me what my dates were for release, etc., and like everyone else, I was escorted to my house for the next, theoretically, three years. In my case, that was a lower bunk in a large barracks building in the fenced compound.

Conscientious objectors were not grouped together or separated from the other prisoners, and that definitely made for a more interesting experience. My upper berth bunkmate, Ray, was a very pleasant black fellow who, like many of the other prisoners, wound up in a federal prison because his offense, which I can't recall, while not especially significant, involved federal property. Although we had very little in common beyond our present situation, we spent a lot of time in pleasant arguments about nothing in particular, especially about the wording of poems and songs we both thought we were experts on. I will always remember his insistence on, "You got to accent the positive, Relent the negative!" When I challenged him, he spelled it out clearly, but he never convinced me he was right. (I still think it's supposed to be "Eliminate the negative," isn't it?)

We actually had quite a bit of freedom within the barbed wire confines of our compound as long as we were where we were supposed to be when we were supposed to be there, such as bedtime, mealtime, and work assignment time. Our guards, derisively called "screws," made regular counts several times a day. Much of our spare time was spent reading, visiting with other conscientious objectors, or in the recreation area. There was a commissary where we could purchase sundries with any money that had been deposited into our account by friends or relatives. The same building housed the mess hall and the administrative staff.

Frank Trieste and Al Orcutt, the two conscientious objectors who had been sentenced to two years on the same day I received my three-year term, were among the men I often visited. Others I remember offhand include Bob Lam, Lawrence Stickney, Amos Brokaw, Loren "Stubby" Watts, someone with the last name Pierce, someone with the first name Bruce, and one other, someone with whom I had a lot of very pleasant talks but surprisingly whom I cannot recall the name of now.

It was also entertaining at times to listen to some of the other inmates swap stories. One fellow swore he knew who had squealed on him, and he knew how he was going to get him when he got out. Mind you, this was before the movie *Fargo*, so obviously, he had the idea first. But out on the ranch where this guy worked was this huge machine for grinding horse meat into some kind of feed. "Hamboig, nuttin' but hamboig," he'd say. "Dat's all 'at'll be left of him"! Many of the stories, of course, involved "innocent" men wrongly convicted, and I must admit some of them sounded pretty convincing. There was also the aged Indian who was exempted from bed counts and other restrictions. The guards told us he had completed his sentence or was at least long ago qualified for parole for killing in Arizona territory before it became a state in 1912. But he had no place to go and the island was his home. He was simply allowed to stay there.

One exception to the general integration of the prisoners in the barracks was the large contingency of Nisei, or second-generation Japanese. These men (boys), drafted from the internment camps in which Roosevelt had ordered all West Coast Japanese confined, were not pacifists but refused induction while they and their families were thus

illegally deprived of their rights. A large number of them were assigned to the kitchen and food preparation duties, but others worked with the rest of the inmates, and we all freely associated during unsupervised time. Being—in our minds—not criminals but men of conscience, we found much in common, and often close friendships developed. Such was the case with Kazuki Hirose and me. Unfortunately, the saddest incident in my time at McNeil involved one of the most popular of Nisei, Fred Irye. Fred was assigned to work in the electrical substation for the camp and was electrocuted because of a crack in the insulation on the handle of a power switch he was told to pull! I later had a chance to see where it happened and can never forget the blackened and chipped spots of concrete on the floor where the current went down through the nails in the bottom of his boots. Just recently, on a television documentary on the internment of the Japanese during the war, his picture was shown as the one fatality among those who had been imprisoned for refusing induction from the internment camps.

Daily camp routine, not counting a during-the-night bed count, began with breakfast. We were then loaded in small groups into covered trucks, along with a couple of guards and transported out to our work locations. For some, these were the cattle barns, chicken barns, or the like. My friend Kaz and I often found ourselves on the same work detail, and we found many ways to have fun without getting into trouble. I recall working with him in the garden patch, hoeing, weeding, etc. But especially, I remember some happy times picking Bing Cherries and Delicious Apples. We'd hang out for the better part of the day in some inconspicuous tree enjoying almost as much fruit as we turned in. We seemed to hit it off really well with a guard named Fifield whose main concern was that we remain accounted for and not become a burden to him.

Fruit and eggs that could be smuggled into the barracks were in demand and were often used to barter for contraband or commissary items. A couple of enterprising fellows in one barracks made applejack using a mop bucket and wringer to squeeze the juice, adding raisins and allowing it to ferment.

A landmark of sorts we frequently passed on our way to the fields was Boot Hill, where prisoners were buried who had no family to claim them. There were only fifteen or twenty simple markers, but there was always one open grave waiting for the next pine box. When someone was buried, a new grave was dug, and that dirt was used to fill the one just used.

It had never been my intention to be a resistor, or troublemaker at Mc-Neil. I felt that I had made my statement in refusing to acquiesce to military conscription, which in my mind was rendering unto Caesar that which is God's, and that prison was an acceptable, if distasteful, consequence of that decision.

Now prison life, even at its finest—which this was far from (or should it be "from which this was far"?)—is pretty distasteful. Of course, there were reportedly those for whom life was so miserable that they had deliberately destroyed government property or violated other federal laws to enjoy the comparative luxury of life at McNeil. A verse I have always liked is, "Stone walls do not a prison make, / Nor iron bars a cage, / Minds innocent and quiet take/ That for a hermitage; / If I have freedom in my love / And in my soul am free, / Angels alone; that soar above, / Enjoy such liberty." (From Lovelace's "To Althea, from Prison"). Not for me! I was not mistreated; was well-fed and adequately clothed; had books to read, and friends with whom to talk; and could send and receive limited mail (three to seven approved people), albeit censored; but the loss of freedom was still a dreadful experience! Prison camp was bad enough. I had no wish to be confined to a cell in the Big House. Nonetheless, I came precipitously close to that fate on several occasions.

I still could not bring myself to cooperate gracefully with an authoritarian system such as, I guess, a prison has to be. So I often failed to comply promptly with instructions given to me and was frequently threatened with dire consequences. When I was finally called to Camp Director Stevens' office, his primary complaint was that my tactics were being too well-received by my fellow inmates, and that he could not allow such a breakdown in discipline. He certainly didn't want to have to send me down, he said, but what, he asked, was he to do? I agreed I didn't want to go either, but of course, the decision was for him to make. Actually, it appeared they really didn't want my type in the Big House, possibly because such non-violent resistance is harder for them to deal with and would be a problem if it spread. So he eventually asked me what I would like to do;—go to the kitchen; work in the library; or wash windows and do general clean-up work there in the office? I left the choice up to him. He finally sent me back to where I was, but only after pleading with me to please be more cooperative and not make him have to take more drastic action. And things continued on pretty much as they had been.

As I approached the end of my first year at McNeil, I naturally applied for a third-of-term parole, even though it was commonly understood that such was not generally given to conscientious objectors. So I was disappointed, but not surprised, when my application was denied by whatever parole board was responsible for such things. I was surprised, though, when a week later I was told to report to get a haircut and fitted for a suit! The very next day, I was dressed out in new clothes, given an overcoat and hat, and sent to the warden's office. He personally handed me the customary $15.00 given with the new clothes to each person released (supposedly enough to get him somewhere and start a crime-free life on the outside). But in my case, I also got an airline ticket to the Harford-Springfield Airport, and a free trip to the airport! I never quite understood how my father arranged it, but somehow, he pulled strings and sent the ticket to the warden, and the red-tape disappeared. I believe Freda and her crew were working behind the scenes. One very happy young man arrived home on Thanksgiving Eve, 1946!

It was still a form of parole, of course, and I arranged to have my college psychology professor, Dr. Howard Spoerl, become my parole advisor for the two years remaining on my sentence. He was a pacifist also and acted as a parole advisor in name only, although I did have to have his approval to get married, which occurred on the following Thanksgiving Day!

NICK MIGLIORINO

Nick (left) interviewed May 10, 2005 by Marcus Rosenbaum,

Author's photo

"Conscientious objectors had a difficult time after the war. There were plenty of job openings but no one would hire us. Feelings against COs were strong. I had to support myself and my family, so I suppose you could say I went underground. If someone asked me about my war experience, I simply told them I had served. When I retired, I began to think about my CPS experience. I wrote a book called *The Lost Illusion* (unpublished) because we entered CPS on the basis of an illusion which was false. We were to do work of national importance. In the early months, we all went to meditation and we worked hard. We wanted the program to succeed.

"Then we began to realize we weren't doing work of national importance. We were sent to work in out-of-the-way places to perform 'make work projects.' To be allowed to do this pretend work, our families or churches had to pay the government $35.00/month. Many of us became discouraged.

"A newspaper circulated in the camp that General Hershey had testified at a congressional hearing. He had called CPS a salvage operation. Lew Ayres, the actor in *All Quiet on the Western Front* (acclaimed first antiwar film of the sound era, winner of awards), was a conscientious objector at a CPS camp who did join the military. It was Hershey's hope that we would also be salvaged, that we would be persuaded to change our minds.

"I was born in 1920 in Peterson, New Jersey, during the Spanish Influenza Epidemic. I came down with the flu and the doctors had given up on me, but not my mother. She took me to the church and placed me before the statue of St. Francis. She dedicated me to St. Francis. She wanted me to be a priest, and so I was raised a Catholic.

"When I was in high school preparing for my confirmation, the sister sent me in to see the monsignor. She said I was disturbing the class with my questions. I had begun to read Voltaire and Rousseau, the Age of Enlightenment philosophies and politics.

"Among other things, this philosophy was based on the thesis that truth should be determined by reason and factual analysis, not faith, dogma, or religious training. I became dissuaded about the existence of Hell. How can there be an all-knowing god who created man and knows exactly what he will do, what the faults of man are, knowing he will go wrong, and then send him to eternal Hell?

"Instead of discussing with me, the monsignor scolded me and tried to scare me. So I was no longer a Catholic.

"When I was called up, I went before the draft board to request consideration as a conscientious objector. They said, 'We checked with Father K. and he said you haven't been to his church in five years. How do you respond?'

"I replied, 'I never went to his church. He must have me confused with someone else.'

"The chairman of the draft board said, 'You have too many answers.'

"I was the only one in Patterson who applied for conscientious objector status and they gave it to me.

"In CPS camps, I had the opportunity to have great debates about the Age of Enlightenment and many other philosophes. The Quakers' philosophy or witness was to do good. That was what we thought we were doing originally. We'd get our work done as fast as we could.

"Because of our lost illusion, some of us began the Gandhi phase of nonviolent resistance, total resistance. We began with work slowdowns. Under Selective Service rules, if we refused to work, we went to prison for five years, but we didn't refuse to work. I became an expert with an ax. I could have a foreman standing over me and directing me, and just by the flick of the wrist, by twisting my wrist at the last moment, I could make the axe bounce off a tree. We applauded each other, and the foreman would be swearing at us. It wasn't important if we cut the tree down or not, actually. After a while, it didn't matter. So every once in a while, someone would get up and go over and hit the tree with the ax.

"When Germfask opened, Colonel Kosch said, 'Now we have all the rotten apples in one basket.'" And he came up to look at the basket.

"Tobacco Road was one of the camp barracks that was absolutely contrary to every regulation. When the colonel came to visit, we plastered the whole barracks with toilet paper.

"He went to dinner with us, and I happened to be on the kitchen work committee. Everything had to be exactly prepared. We sliced the potatoes carefully; the meat had to be sliced to perfection. We worked diligently, making everything perfect until it became quite late. Finally, he went stamping out without dinner.

"I was a writer. Before I was drafted, I went to New York University and took classes in fiction writing while working as a copy boy at a newspaper. There were two major pacifist groups at that time, the Fellowship of Reconciliation, and the War Resisters League, a secular organization. I became a correspondent for the War Resisters League. I began to write letters about our unpaid forced labor camps. I began to get some response.

"Reporters came to Germfask. They asked me, 'Why don't you leave camp?' I replied, 'Are you saying I shouldn't follow Selective Service rules?' I didn't walk out to go to prison as some conscientious objectors did.

"*Time* magazine came out with a story about Germfask. Some of us collectively wrote a rebuttal editorial back which they published. Our rebuttal stated the real story is America's first experiment without pay in forced labor camps. I was the first one to sign it, so my name was on top. And that was enough. I shortly received notice that I had become religiously insincere. The general ordered my local draft board to induct me into the service.

"I appeared before them. The entire hearing consisted of the chairman standing up and saying, 'The general really has a hard on for you, and if the general wants your ass, he'll get no objection from us.' I was reclassified 1-A, available for draft.

"I appealed. Frieda Lazarus, Richard Lazarus' mother, from the War Resisters League, arranged my defense.

"In the final appeals to the President and the director of Selective Service, General Hershey sits in the President's place at the hearing. He is in a position of absolute power. He filed a complaint against me, and now he was to judge my hearing. I would have to appear before him personally, and he would decide my case.

"Somehow, I did not appear before Hershey. Someone sat in his place. My attorney said, 'The FBI has really done a complete job on you.'

"During the hearing, I was asked, 'When you were in the fourth grade, your classmates asked you to contribute ten cents to the Red Cross and you did not participate; how do you answer the charge?'

"There was a candy store near the school and I never spent a dime there, I never had a dime. So I replied, 'Did the FBI check to see whether I had a dime?'

"I had a difficult time trying to convince these military minds that even during a time of war, citizens do not lose their constitutional rights. The judge said he didn't see anything in writing from Selective Service allowing denial of constitutional rights. I won my case. The judge actually ruled against his military superior.

"Later, I asked Richard whether Frieda had somehow arranged for this particular judge for my hearing. It was then I found out he was not a career officer but a reserve officer and a noted constitutional lawyer.

"Richard just smiled and said, 'That's the way she operates.'

"After the war, we all went different ways. I came back to New York. Many of us became underground men from our Germfask experience in order to secure work. The concept of organized resistance to war had not evolved, so we would not have been accepted.

"I kept thinking about my experience at Germfask and the kind of witness we thought we were making. I thought about the Quakers' witness and I thought about our witness of Gandhi's nonresistance.

"I hung out at the Hall of Nations on 5th Avenue. This was where pacifists met and the modern pacifist movement started in the United States. There I met Bayard Rustin, a World War II CO. He was the man who twenty years later organized the march in Washington, D.C. for racial equality for Martin Luther King. And, he is the one who is historically given credit for having persuaded Martin Luther King to adopt the non-violent Gandhi technique we adopted in Germfask.

"He and Martin Luther King took a basic political philosophy and combined it with a social movement. They combined that aspect of pacifism with racial equality. They combined a political movement with an acceptable social institution. At Germfask, we were lacking that social institution that made our movement meaningful. The American public would not have accepted it.

"After the war, I returned to Patterson and wrote for the Patterson newspaper, a daily newscast for a radio station, and scripts for a hand puppet troupe. I returned to New York where Harold Keller and I opened our own public relations agency. He was the public relations manager for Tom Dewey and Dwight Eisenhower. We developed several subsidiaries and grew into a coast-to-coast corporation. I retired and now live in Florida."

ARDEN BODE

May 11, 2005 Interview

"Being a conscientious objector during World War II was extremely emotionally expensive, but it was the right decision for me. I had to clam up my emotions to do it. Twenty-five years later, I finally started to un-clam. I didn't have to go into CPS; I qualified for the seminary. I had taken all the courses in philosophy and religion. I chose CPS because it was the right decision for me. It was emotional intelligence.

"I was in four CPS camps in fourteen months. The last two were La Pine and Germfask. It was in Germfask that I had the opportunity to meet Danny Dingman, Neubrand, Partridge, and other men with great character. **Al Partridge and some other conscientious objectors started KPFA, America's first listener-supported alternative radio station**.

"Sometimes we played touch football, but the work was emotional torture. Our job was to drain a swamp, refill it, and then drain it again.

"I walked out of Germfask about December 23, was arrested, and sentenced to federal prison in Ashland, Kentucky, for just under two years. Most of the prisoners were convicted Kentucky moonshiners. The prison was segregated, and even though I was white, I was moved into the black area. I liked it much better there. I was more accepted by the prisoners and I could listen to good blues and jazz instead of country music. **Bayard Rustin was one of my fellow inmates.** Rustin demonstrated passive non-violent resistance in India with Mahatma Gandhi. He later became a mentor to Martin Luther King, Jr. and helped King organize the Southern Christian Leadership Conference.

"Rustin and I were two of several inmates at Ashland to demonstrate against the segregated federal prison system.

"After the war, I moved to Florida. During the building boom, I was known as the cement man of Miami. I was the major supplier of precast stones.

"Several years ago, I moved to Whittier, California to be near my daughter. I have been active in passive protests since World War II. I protested this current war. I was just released from the hospital for abdominal surgery, an aneurism, a dangerous surgery. My doctor said not to go to the protest, but I did it anyway. I sat in the middle of the boulevard in a wheelchair next to a man who was protesting the protesters. The protesters didn't understand why I was conversing with a man who didn't agree with them. I paid a price in the antiwar community for being friends with a man who protested the protesters. And none of these people saw the humor in this.

"I listen to all people's opinions. Why should I be enemies with this man because he disagrees with me? He has been my friend for many years. The theoretical position of pacifists is that you do not make enemies with people who have different opinions from you."

RICHARD LAZARUS MEMOIR

Richard Lazarus was the son of Frieda Lazarus, the antiwar activist mentioned earlier in this book.

Memories of Civilian Public Service Camps

April 2006

For a long time, I've been thinking of making a record of my stay in the camps for conscientious objectors during World War II. Recently, I have been in contact with Danny Dingman, a former campmate, who sent me a paper that he had written about his experiences, so I decided to do the same.

Back in 1940, President Roosevelt was manipulating to get the United States into the war going on with France and England against Germany. He got Congress to pass the Selective Service Act.

As required, I registered in July of 1941, stating in my registration that I was a conscientious objector. Some months later, I got orders from my draft board to appear for induction and I applied for Form 47 to state my reason for being a conscientious objector. As far as my training was concerned, the family had been pacifist for a long time. My mother had been a member of the Women's Peace Union and the War Resisters League. She was also a Women's Peace Union delegate to the disarmament conference held in Geneva, Switzerland, in 1932. I was able to show from readings such as *All Quiet on the Western Front* that I had been trained to be a conscientious objector.

As far as religious beliefs, I believed that a common spirit went through all of humanity. I didn't believe in a Supreme Being that directed the destiny of people. I just felt that we're all on the same planet and we all belong to one another. I had this mantra that wars will cease when men refuse to fight.

The local board asked me, "What would you do if your mother, sister, or grandmother were being raped?" Now this is a foolish question since war is organized killing—they use airplanes to bomb people and poisonous gas to kill people. What did that have to do with me as an individual? Besides, what could I do if someone held a gun to my head or a knife to my throat? However, the local board turned down my application. I had to write within ten days to make an appeal to Washington, D.C., which I did, reiterating the same reasons I had given my local draft board. They also wanted some kind of character reference. I told them I had returned some money wrongly given to me by a ticket agent selling tickets to the play *Hamlet.* The ticket seller was so impressed that she gave me a free ticket to the play. I used this incident as my character reference and I was classified IV-E, conscientious objector status. I was ordered to Big Flats, New York. This former CCC camp was under the auspices of the Society of Friends (Quakers).

At first, the Quakers, Mennonites, and Brethren thought they would be running these camps primarily for their own constituents. They had some idea that they were going to engage in Foreign Service work. *The Story of CPS*, a book published by the Mennonites, states that Selective Service quickly set them straight. Colonel Kosch told them in no uncertain terms, "You are managers. We run the program and you do what we tell you."

Colonel Franklin McLean brought that out in strong language when he said, "The program is not carried out for the education of the individual, to train groups for Foreign Service or future activities in the post-war period, or the furtherance of any particular movement." He further said, "The assignees had certain rights and were only granted privileges. These privileges could be restricted or withdrawn without consent as punishment during an emergency or in a manner of policy. We may tell them where to work, what to wear, and where to sleep."

So you would think that when such strong language was put out by Selective Service, the religious agencies would say, "Well, we're not running these camps under those circumstances."

It shows how naïve these religious organizations were. If they had refused to participate under such conditions, there would have been different arrangements. In England, conscientious objectors were given individual assignments, and Canada, which started the work camp program, dropped it and followed the English model.

I received my notice to report to camp and a list of what to bring: a whole set of clothing, my own toiletries, and my own sheets. In addition, I was expected to pay $35.00 a month to maintain myself at camp. From the $35.00, we were paid $2.50 a month.

At one point, I had some idea of refusing to register and at another point refusing to go to camp, but I must say my thoughts were not clear, so I just went along with the prescribed program.

When I arrived in camp, everything was in turmoil. Stanley Murphy, George Willoughby, and Lou Taylor walked out to protest against conscription and how the camps were being run by the religious agencies. This was the first time anyone had left a camp voluntarily, and instead, had chosen the consequence of going to prison. Their actions upset many people.

There was also talk about going on strike because of the $2.50 a month wages. I never paid the $35.00, but I collected the $2.50 whenever possible. I realized the talk about a strike was only talk. Some of them were anti-union. These religious fundamental guys had a nice nest and they just wanted to sit the war out and study their Bible. One time I asked a guy, "What is God?" He said, "That's one of them there college questions." I must say that's a joke because it makes me feel a little superior, which I feel guilty about.

Anyway, I'll give you an example of how their people were willing not to cause waves. I'd been there about three months when the project superintendent complained to Selective Service about low productivity. Selective Service sent a telegram informing the director that it would be taking over. This caused the director to panic. He called a meeting and informed the assignees they had to put in an honest day's work. What is an honest day's work? We're there under coercion, we're working for peanuts, we're held accountable to Selective Service for twenty-four hours a day, and we can't leave camp unless we have permission. So where is the honest day's work connected to that?

During this meeting, another thing that came up, which I had never heard of before but was quite prevalent in society, was the concept of precedent. Namely, that you're arguing about something that happened ten, fifty, or one hundred years ago and that sets a precedent about what's happening today. So the administration said that if Selective Service took over our camp, it would set a precedent to take over other camps. We voted. Sixty-five men swore they would be good guys, honest workers. Five of us voted against it, and I was one of the five. Needless to say, there wasn't really much improvement in the work.

I originally had been quite keen on soil conservation. In fact, I was on the civilian service list as a junior soil conservationist with a job offer in Alabama, but I was drafted first. I was one of the few people there who believed the work was of national importance, but coercion and conscription overrode those feelings.

A few weeks before Christmas, word was received that the stores in El-mira were looking for people to hire for packing, sales, and various other jobs because of a dearth of labor. About twenty of us went to work for different salaries. Since we were all in the same boat, I suggested we take the pay, put it in a pot, and divide it equally. That idea was turned down vociferously. It just showed me there was no common feeling among the conscientious objectors. They were just individuals who couldn't join to-gether in any common venture. In religious camps, you couldn't trust the men. Whereas in Germfask, to get ahead of my story, men were supportive of one another.

In the spring, I volunteered for an opening at a side camp in Ohio for planting trees as flood control. At this camp were several men who were against conscription: Jack McGraw, Jim Bristol, Milton Kramer, Joe Guin, Wally Nelson, and me. We decided that we were going to walk out in pro-test. We wrote letters to all the camps and tried to get them to join us in a mass walk-out.

I went home on furlough, intending not to go back, and that made real turmoil at my home. My father felt that if I went to prison, I would always have a low status and never get a job. My mother felt it might interfere with her work. She was working with government officials to get a number of men out of prison and paroled to CPS. A lot of pressure was put on me, so I went back to camp. The men I mentioned above were still in camp, but they later walked out. They were tolerant and didn't say anything about my return. In fact, Milton Kramer and I were friends right up until he died about 1996.

When I arrived back in camp, I was very depressed, but my eventual feeling was "Life is an adventure," so I was able to overcome my depres-sion and went to work. In late October, I bruised my foot and couldn't walk very well, so I was in sick quarters. In sick quarters were two men who were really sick. They were classed as conscientious objectors, but the doctor should have classified them IV-F (medical discharge). Doc-tors had no sympathy for conscientious objectors. I talked to the men and thought to myself, *I'm really not suited mentally for this work; I should get a IV-F too.* They gave me some of their pills that would keep me awake, but I didn't take them until late in December.

In the meantime, I wrote a letter to Colonel Kosch.

Dear Colonel Kosch:

October 7ᵗʰ marked my completion of one year in the civilian public service system, and as is my custom, I am reflecting on that year. What has been the value of that experience and what does it presage for the future? Has it been the building ground for creative pioneering? No, I think not. I find the creative me must be free. Creations are merely the visible forms, the material forms of a state of mind. The Egyptian slaves working on the pyramids didn't create; they were machines, blindly doing their master's bidding. Only free humans can create. Has the work performed been that of national importance? Some has, yes, but I have never performed. If a job requires fifty men and there are one hundred men at hand to do the work of fifty, then fifty of those men are boondoggling. That has been the history of my work in CPS. I have been an extra unneeded man. No, I find that my experience in camp has been of value whenever I and others whom I have been able to influence have caused trouble to the officials of the soil conservation service, the American Friends Service, and the Selective Service System. Our fast on behalf of Gandhi achieved publicity in newspapers from coast to coast. That is the kind of experience I'm going to encourage as much a possible this coming year. I shall continue to be as obnoxious as possible to the project men. In that way, I can get them mad at the assignees to achieve greater unity. Many assignees wonder whether the civilian public service system, because of its boondoggling, has made them unfit for work. I do not think that. Before being assigned to camp, I never held a job for more than four months. I seemed to be psychologically unsuited to discipline, but now I have a steady job. That job is to make the civilian public service system as uncomfortable as I can for the officials.

Sincerely,

Richard Lazarus

Colonel Kosch did not reply; however, Mary Newman from the American Friends Service Committee sent a letter to the director of Selective Service saying it couldn't make me repent by ordering me to a government camp, that being my chief desire since the previous June.

At Big Flats, about twenty-one of us decided to support Gandhi's non-violent protest by going on a hunger strike. The first day we went to work with no breakfast and refused lunch. As soon as the administration learned we refused to eat, it called us in and we spent the rest of the day in our bunks. We refused to eat supper. Seventeen of the men decided to call one day sufficient to prove our point, but four of us decided we would fast for three days: John Yanger, Eugene Collier, Tad Tekla, and myself. We fasted for three days and there was no harm. I felt fine.

About ten days later, Colonel McLean came along and interviewed the four of us, individually. When he called me up, I refused to go. When I was called up the second time, I went, reluctantly. In hindsight, I wish I wouldn't have gone. Evidently, the administration hadn't made a record of the seventeen men who fasted and he wanted their names. He thought there was some kind of conspiracy going on. Neither I nor the other three told him anything. I just gave him facetious answers. I suppose he was going to give everyone involved black marks.

Now to get back to those pills. In December, I took the pills, and for three or four days, I didn't sleep and ate sparingly. I collapsed at work and was put into sick quarters, where I decided I would become paranoid. I set up a system that allowed only my friends to see me. I did it by running strings to the door lock. I could manipulate the lock by pulling the strings. The camp physician told me he was sorry that he couldn't handle my case. My mother and sister came and told me I looked terrible. They took me to Chicago, where they were living at the time. I was sent to the Cook County Psychiatric Hospital. All of us patients lived in a big dorm.

There were elderly senile men who incurred the wrath of the attendants who put them in straitjackets. All night long, these men would be moaning in pitiful voices, "Please let me out." It was distressing, but somehow, I managed to get some sleep. There were also men sent here for observation who had been in the army. Some of them were very hostile and didn't want anyone coming near them. They needed a certain space. And then there were the pranksters. They were always making jokes. The psychiatrists threw up their hands because they would tell one story one day and another story the next day. These men were very happy-go-lucky. They seemed to take nothing seriously, and I guess that's how they regarded the army. They never dressed properly, were always slovenly, didn't salute properly, and if they happened to be put in the guard house for some infraction, they thought it was a joke.

So, I thought to myself, *well, that's a great way to resist the army. Make everything a joke like the good soldier Schweik, a Czech soldier in the Austrian Army.* After ten days in that hospital, I was released, but not before I had a bad experience. I was given a spinal tap to determine whether I had syphilis. It gave me the worst headache I'd ever had, one I can still remember today.

Years later, when I visited the peace collection at Swarthmore College, I read the letter the hospital superintendent had written to Selective Service. It said, "In my opinion, he is a schizoid personality who may have had an acute psychotic episode which subsided in a short time."

After I got out of the hospital, I worked in Chicago. At the end of February, a letter came from Selective Service ordering me to appear before the medical advisory board. On that board was a woman psychiatrist who strongly supported the war. She evidently concurred with the superintendent's opinion because, a week later, I received a letter ordering me to return to camp. (In support of the Quakers, they had been trying to get me a IV-F but Selective Service overrode it.)

I reported back to Big Flats and then was ordered to Mancos, Colorado. I was given vouchers to travel. The trip was interesting. I went from Alamosa to Durango, Colorado, by way of a narrow gauge train. We traveled through the mountains. I could look out the window and see the track running along a cliff with a chasm below. I understand that today it is a tourist attraction.

From Durango, I took a bus to Mancos. The Mancos project was to build a collection basin for the Mancos River. My job was to bang nails into slats that went into forms, which didn't take much energy.

I didn't like some of the conscientious objectors in this camp. They were also very boisterous and loud. Their idea of humor was to give someone a hot foot, and they hogged the pool table. One of them, an assistant police chief in some town in Texas, actually brought boxing gloves to the camp. He wanted Ralph Polliam and me to fight. Ralph was a short guy like me. It was a foolish idea and I refused.

They were mostly Southern fundamentalists. Some men felt they were more sincere than others. The Quakers, especially, looked down on the non-religious and the philosophical objectors, such as myself. It was like George Orwell; some people are more equal than others, and some people are more sincere than others. I thought this was foolish. If a person is willing to take the ostracism of the community, he may not be as verbal as college-educated people, but he can be just as sincere. What I used to do in the evening at suppertime was to sit at the table with the administration staff. I never said anything, just sat there in silence. I let my beard and hair grow. At first, one of the loutish foreman said something about nasty Jews and made nasty remarks, but I just disregarded it. After a few days, they disregarded me, and I just sat there quietly in rebuke, or what I thought was rebuke.

Camp Germfask

I had been in Mancos less than two months when we got word that a camp was opening in Germfask, Michigan. I was one of about ten sent from Mancos. Men from other camps were also sent there.

I really liked Germfask because everyone was accepted as they were. There was no judgment that this guy was better than that guy.

So in Germfask, there was discussion, as in all camps, about walking out; however, my thinking had changed. I felt to walk out was a mistake. We'd be sacrificing ourselves to the government, and it could in that way quiet us. I felt it was more important to continue what we were doing, resisting conscription by a method of slowdown and obstruction. That was our method of combating conscription, like the good soldier Schweik, the Czech soldier in the Austrian army who constantly misunderstood orders.

My first job at Germfask was as night watchman and the man in charge of the stoves. Even though it was May, it was chilly, and I was to make sure the pot-bellied stoves in the dorms were filled with coal and shaken down so the ashes would drop to the bottom. Later, I was to raise the alarm if we were invaded by people hostile to conscientious objectors, which never happened.

The only thing that did happen, antagonistic to conscientious objectors, was when a camp group drove to Newberry, a nearby city, and was harassed by a group of local citizens, lumberjacks, who ordered them to leave town. Evidently, one man, Al Partridge, had a big black beard. That seemed to annoy them, inflame them. He tried talking to the aroused citizenry but to no effect. So about 150 irate citizens gathered around the truck, but the conscientious objectors left without any real harm occurring.

You must remember that some of those conscientious objectors and the Jehovah's Witnesses were pretty big guys, and the Jehovah's Witnesses were not pacifists. They were in CPS because they wanted the ministerial classification. Every Jehovah's Witness claimed he was a minister. If they weren't granted that classification, they refused to go into the army. A great many of them went to jail. I would say of the 6,000 war protesters who were in jail, maybe half of them were Jehovah's Witnesses.

So I was a night watchman, which gave me a lot of time for reading. The local library was cooperative and brought in a lot of books, and interestingly, when the camp closed, every book was accounted for but one. I gave up the night watchman job because I felt, *Let somebody else have a chance at it*, and I went out on the project on the refuge.

I got along very well with the project foreman, Harvey Saunders. In fact, he told me that after the war, he wanted me to go with him to Canada to work in a logging camp. I don't know why he had that idea because I was a very poor producer, although I had a lot of previous experience with an axe and saw from working on the Dutch Elm Commission before going into CPS.

One time I challenged Mr. Saunders to a chopping contest. My salary of a nickel a day (we had gotten an increase in salary, now $5.00 a month) against his day salary. I don't know what he got. Well, it took me about four minutes to go through this log and then he picked another one comparable in size and bang, bang, bang. In one minute, he was through the log. I gave him a nickel and he gave me a candy bar.

Saunders liked the men, even though he didn't agree with them and didn't like their work habits. But what he did like was there was no swearing on the project, and the men weren't drunks, maybe only an occasional overdrinking. Also, none of the guys were violent toward one another. One time, I got a lift from an ex-soldier, a veteran, who asked me specifically about that, whether there were fights, and I told him no, there were never fights.

The other foreman really hated us and quit after a month or so. Then he wrote an article for *The American Legion Magazine*; this man was a discharged veteran, telling about what slackers we were and how we were incorrigible. His article led to an article in the *Detroit Free Press* with a big headline in red letters, "Camp Chiefs Powerless in Revolt by Objectors."

At this time, we had several arrests, including Don DeVault. He refused to work on the duck ponds and stayed in the dorm doing penicillin research. He was arrested and charged with desertion, even though he was in camp.

The administration told the town operator not to allow any telephone calls or telegrams, but I was able to sneak out of camp and hitchhike to Blaney Park where I sent a telegram to *The Conscientious Objector*, the newspaper for the War Resisters League. My mother got word of it and notified the American Civil Liberties Union, and we had a big to-do. Don was given a three-year prison sentence.

In October, Jack Hood was arrested for taking government-issued clothes out of camp. Marvin Cook was arrested for supposedly obtaining an illegal trapping license.

In addition to the *American Legion Magazine* article and the *Detroit Free Press* article, the local district attorney made lying remarks in the local newspaper, probably to get himself some political enhancement. He accused the conscientious objectors of rioting at the camp, making insulting remarks and unsolicited advances to women in Manistique, and looking for what he called "victory girls." He was backed up by a minister of a local church. It developed that two men had been attending the minister's church, and they had asked three high school girls whether they wanted to go to the movies. The girls had refused. These two men were married and that made the minister sure that they were breaking their vows and wanted to seduce the girls. Evidently, one of the conscientious objectors had angered this minister by questioning a theosophical interpretation of the Bible the minister had made. Owen Knox, a minister from St. Claire, Michigan, who was a member of the Fellowship of Reconciliation, came to Manistique and questioned the district attorney and the ministers of the town. The district attorney could not bring a single instance to back up any of his charges and all the other ministers said they got along fine with the conscientious objectors. He was the only minister who objected. It was really a tempest started by this district attorney. **However, *Time* magazine picked up on the story and repeated the charges that the district attorney had made. We wrote letters explaining that these things were not true and pointing out that the real issue was conscription.**

I was distressed that somebody had gone into the storage area where the food was kept, broken the lock, and knocked over some jars of mustard, ripped open a bag of beans, and did some other small damage. If they were really going to trash the place, they would have done a lot more damage. I felt it was a lack of discipline and we had been disciplined in our slowdown. We had not done any physical damage to the property. We had refrained from breaking anything. I thought this was bad; it was the beginning of a breakdown, and non-violent resistance has to have discipline. It has to be individual discipline, not necessarily group discipline.

All this publicity was causing a furor to have the camp removed. Everyone in the camp agreed; we wanted it removed. We wanted to be discharged.

I would like to mention an incident that happened to me. In January, I saw a notice in the Escanaba newspaper that the Don Cossacks, a performing Russian troupe, were going to give a concert. I wrote for a ticket, and on the day of the performance, a Saturday, I left camp without furlough papers or passes. The only time I requested those passes was if I would be on a long furlough out of state. I walked to Blaney Park, got a bus, and went to Escanaba and saw the performance, which was great. I was disappointed that the chorus, instead of being young soldiers, were men in their late fifties, but they had beautiful voices. During intermission, I got up and walked around. There were about 200 people who left their seats, but I was surprised when they didn't talk to one another. It was so different from New York where everybody gets up to circulate and talk. With these people, it was almost as if they were there as a matter of duty, something they had to do, but they weren't really enjoying it.

After the performance, about 10 p.m., I had a choice of waiting for the bus, which would come at 5 a.m., or starting to walk back the seventy-five miles, figuring I might get a lift. I did get a lift from a high school teacher who had seen me in the audience. He took me about fifteen miles to where there was a road junction and I started walking. I figured I could do four miles in an hour, and by five hours or so, I would be twenty miles to the next town. If it looked favorable, I might wait there or continue walking. Well, I'd been waiting about an hour when along came a milk truck on its way to Manistique and Blaney Park. The driver welcomed me as somebody he could talk to while he was driving. He said he usually got rather lonely. We got to Manistique and I went around with him while he made his deliveries. When we arrived at Blaney Park, I got off and walked back to camp. I was back about 2 a.m. and had enjoyed the night.

To get back to my story, we're now into April. In April, I saw a notice in the paper that there was a sunrise service in Manistique. Although I'm not religious, I thought it would be interesting. Danny Dingman, Bent Andresen, and I bought round-trip bus tickets.

After the service, we were eating breakfast when a state trooper arrested us and took us to the local jail. We were held incommunicado. The next day, Danny looked out the window and saw a high school girl from Germfask, who attended our movies, getting off the bus. He called to her to get in touch with his brother back at camp, which she did. We were in the Manistique jail for two or three days. The food was very good. The jailer's wife was a great cook. But the wheels were set in motion. We were taken to Marquette, the federal holding place. We were brought before the local magistrate and he let go on our own recognizance. We didn't have to put up any bail. We were free. I went to New York and got a job. I think I worked for about two months.

In the meantime, my mother was working out a deal with the attorney general in Michigan. Since we had return tickets, it showed we did not intend to desert. The attorney general was upset and tired of us because of the number of cases we were bringing before his court. Besides the ten habeas corpus cases, there were about twenty-seven others.

Some conscientious objectors walked out of Germfask in protest of conscription. These were the really courageous guys I admired greatly: Al Partridge, Morris Horowitz, John Neubrand, and Corbett Bishop. Then later, Danny Dingman and Bent Andresen walked out when we were transferred to a camp in Minersville, California, after Germfask had been closed. You have to give them credit for being courageous, but I felt it was now a mistake, that we should have stayed in CPS and made as much noise as possible.

I'd like to mention another man who walked out: George Yamada. George was a Japanese-American who grew up on a sugar beet farm in Nebraska. When he was drafted, he was sent to a CPS camp. When the order came up for all Japanese to go to relocation camps, George was ordered to go. This was one time all the campers showed a unified spirit. Even the Quaker camp director protested. I think everyone in the camp went on strike. The order for George to go was rescinded. At a later time, George was sent to a CPS camp in Colorado. While there, he teamed up with Katherine Brown, a very courageous woman, who is now Katherine Lazarus. They went to a movie and George was ordered to go up into the balcony. He refused, and although Katherine was not arrested, George was arrested for battery, "the offense of equally inciting and stirring up quarrels and suits," a vague charge causing a legal case. The case was dropped and George was sent to Germfask and ultimately walked out.

Transferred to Minersville, California

Germfask closed, a number of men had been discharged, and Danny, Bent, and I were ordered to go to Minersville, by the Trinity River, in northern California. We were to be held there as a reserve for fighting forest fires. There was considerable talk that the Japanese would send over balloons containing incendiary devices to set the forest on fire.

While there, Frank Hatfield and I climbed Mount Shasta. We did a lot of exploring, walking along trails the gold diggers had used for getting water for their diggings. These waterways followed a contour, and it was a lot of fun to walk through the woods. The Trinity River, which must have been a beautiful river at one time, was in horrendous shape because dredgers had dumped stones in the riverbed.

While I was in Minersville, word came that Selective Service was going to use a point system for discharging men. Those who received RTW (Refusal to Work) had minus five points. Since I had fifteen or more RTWs, I was sure I would be held there indefinitely, so I decided to take a gamble. I requested that my papers be sent back to the local draft board, and I was called up for an induction examination. When I was examined, I, of course, passed the physical, but when I came before the psychiatrist, I told him I had been a conscientious objector in a camp for two-and-a-half years but that we conscientious objectors had made a mistake. We should have gone into the army and told the soldiers the war was wrong. Well, he blew his top and underlined that I was unfit for the army and I should be given a IV-F. So I was given a IV-F and was out of the woods, so to speak.

That's the end of my saga.

ICKIER BJORN

July 13, 2005

Dear Mrs. Kopecky,

I think that describing the inmates as refusing to work does not describe us at all. Do you know that we were expected to work for nothing? We were in a slave labor camp and were voicing our objection by refusing to work for nothing. We protested "slave labor" by declining to work. We used passive resistance techniques like Mahatma Gandhi and Jawaharlal Nehru did in India.

We were well-aware of the Russian and German slave labor camps, and we thought the Americans would be embarrassed in admitting that they too had slave labor camps at Mancos, Colorado, La Pine, Oregon, and Germfask, Michigan.

We were paid $5.00 per month for expenses—tobacco, etc. I declined to accept the $5.00 as I had hoped to sue the government for fair wages and I did not wish to prejudice my case by accepting that small amount. But, when released from prison, my attorney advised me not to sue the government while on parole at the risk of being returned to prison.

I was one of the men identified as a recalcitrant at La Pine. John Neubrand and I were ordered by the work superintendent to cut down a certain tree. After giving us instructions, he left us on our own. He drove away along a dead-end road. We felled the tree across the road so he could not drive back to headquarters. He came back and cursed our stupidity. I told him, "It is your carelessness. You should have known that you have reluctant workers; you have to leave someone to supervise that work so that it is done right."

The result was a free trip to Germfask.

There was no animosity in all of this. It was a sort of challenge, and was fun, just as long as they didn't shoot us or "cook" us as they did in Germany and Russia.

While I was in the CPS camps, there were some exceptions to my objections to work. For instance, I would always agree to work where I thought there was an emergency situation. There was a dangerous peat bog fire on the Seney Refuge. I was on hand fighting it. I didn't know what I was doing. At one point, I was surrounded by smoke and fire. Luckily, I had hiked a great number of miles without getting lost, and I think that is what helped me to find safety.

Another situation where I performed slave labor was in the Mancos camp. I was assigned to the laundry and was to hang the clothes to dry. The beneficiaries to this were the inmates of the camp and not the government.

The day before I walked out of Germfask, I noticed an abundance of blueberries. I asked the camp director if I could get two or three men to pick berries for the benefit of the camp personnel. He replied, "I cannot authorize that."

"Well," I said, "this would be one way to get some work from us because it would be for the benefit of the people in camp."

"You win," he said. "Go ahead."

The next day, I was hitchhiking to Portland, Oregon. That, of course, led to my arrest and imprisonment.

John Calef deserted Camp Germfask a few days before me. After dinner, he asked me to walk with him to the bus stop at Blaney Park and help carry his suitcase. It was a ten-mile walk one way. I walked back alone in the dark, getting to camp around midnight. John's family lived in Appleton, Wisconsin, so he didn't have far to go. After prison, he eventually moved to San Francisco, where I met him again.

You may wonder why I would voluntarily exchange Germfask for prison. Was Germfask that bad? Yes, indeed it was. If I had to do it over again, I would do the same thing. We were an educated bunch, and there were no books or libraries at government camps. I enjoyed Balzac's *Droll Stories* and Boccaccio's *Decameron*.

I was sent to the federal prison in Ashland, Kentucky, where I was housed with the segregated blacks. From there, I was transferred to Sandstone Federal Prison in Minnesota. I was assigned to work in the library where I had time to read all of Plato's dialogues, Nietzsche's *Thus Spoke Zarathustra*, Schopenhauer's *The World as Will and Idea,* Santayana's *The Realm of Being*, and John Dewey's *Human Nature and Conduct.* Why did a prison have in its book collections such books? Of course, it was staffed with more popular books such as Zane Grey's westerns.

The conscientious objectors in Selective Service Camps were unusual people with brains. It takes brains to run counter to population. Al Partridge was a university professor, John Neubrand was the youngest person to enroll in Pittsburgh University, up to his time. Morris Horowitz studied at Georgetown University, and Jack Smock was with the University of Washington. George Baird was a track star. He and his fellow runner won the gold medal in the 4 × 400 m relay at the 1928 Summer Olympics. Their record was not broken until the second or third Olympics after World War II.

Roy Kepler arrived after I deserted. He was one of three men who helped raise money to finance conscientious objectors charged with deserting. After the war, Roy, Lew Hill, and Al Partridge, formed radio station KPFA in Berkeley.

One Germfask CO was a researcher in chemistry at Stanford University. He helped perfect penicillin in time to be available for healing World War II soldiers. Don't you wonder whether Selective Service was wrong in taking him from his Stanford laboratory and putting him in Germfask?

When I got to San Francisco after the war, I visited Jack Smock often. I had become interested in hi-fi, operas, and classical music during my stay in prison, and Jack was an expert on hi-fi and electronics. I asked his advice, and he put together the best hi-fi I had ever heard. I was a regular at the opera, ballet, and symphony. It is my belief that I would have missed part of life had I not gone to prison. The prison system provided us with good music. I now have Wagner's seventeen hours of the *Ring of Nibelung* on VHS tapes.

Except for hiking and mountaineering, my first real date with my wife was to take her to see Strauss' Der *Rosenkavalier*. I wanted to ask her to marry me, but she was a three-year World War II veteran, so I did not know how she would react to marrying a conscientious objector. I slipped the ring on her finger as a 105-piece orchestra played *"The Presentation of the Rose,"* a symbol of engagement.

My wife was friends with George Yamada. They went to a movie and he was told to sit in the balcony in the segregated area. They protested and refused. They chose the seats they wanted and weren't kicked out of the theater. He eventually ended up in Germfask.

AL PARTRIDGE: BY PHYLISS PARTRIDGE

2009 Interview

Phyllis Partridge was the second wife of Al Partridge. She shared the following memories.

"Al was one of the men who rode into Newberry in the back of a truck and was the 'Bearded One' in the attempted lynching accounts. He and the other conscientious objectors were confronted with an angry mob. He said he was never so scared in his life. It was the only time he was happy to get back to Germfask.

"Al was in La Pine, Oregon, Mancos, Colorado, and finally Germfask. He walked out of camp and ended up in Ashland Kentucky Penitentiary. He was on parole when we married in 1947. When we met, he told me he'd been a CO during World War II, and I thought he meant 'Commanding Officer.'

"His first wife was pregnant at the time he went into CPS. He was sent to prison and later got divorced.

"Al taught English, drama, and journalism at various universities; at one time he was head of the Broadcast Department at the University of Chicago.

"Al died in 1992, and most of the people Al talked about have died; most notably, Corbett Bishop. I met him a couple of times; eccentric is perhaps too mild a word! The first time I met him, Al and I were standing at a street corner in Chicago. He had a beard and wore something that looked like a robe. He was selling books from the back of a van he was living in. We later visited him at his bookstore in California. A robber entered his store one day and shot and killed him. An ironic ending for a man with strong pacifist beliefs.

"While Al was in Ashland prison, he became distressed over the government's requirement of forced segregation of Negroes. Al was one of the conscientious objectors who went on a hunger strike and was put in isolation for months.

AL'S LETTER OF SEGREGATION PROTEST

Written from Ashland Federal Penitentiary and originally handwritten, with no date or addressee.

Dear Sir:

I had hoped for an opportunity to discuss with you that matter of segregation of Negroes and whites in the dining room; however, you are no doubt too occupied at present to grant an interview so I thought it well to pen you this note.

I am most distressed to discover that a government institution not only permits but requires segregation. Certainly there is little hope of overcoming persecution and intolerance of the Negro if his fundamental rights and equality before the law are not recognized by the very government, or institution of the government which is designated for the public welfare and protection, the public of which the Negro is a recognized member. Concern over this situation makes it impossible for me to continue giving even my licit support to this deplorable policy by continuing to eat in the dining hall where no provision is made for inter-racial eating.

End of Letter

"After prison, Al spent some years as Station Manager of KPFA, Pacifica station founded by Lew Hill and other conscientious objectors. It became the first listener-supported radio broadcaster in the United States. It has many sister stations, including Chicago, New York, and Los Angeles versions. Lew's hope, and Al's, was that they could provide a forum for all viewpoints, including pacifism, and lead to a better world.

Al Partridge, George Reeves, Johnny Calef

Partridge family collection

BACK TO GERMFASK

MAX MACAULAY

June 2005

Left: Max Macaulay 2005, Author's photo Right: Max as a young boy with the bike the conscientious objectors modified and repaired for him. (Susan Macaulay picture)

Max lived his entire life in the Germfask area where he was a respected and successful businessman, farmer, and dedicated family man. At the time of the interview, his father was deceased. Max passed away in September 2014.

Max's dad was a work foreman at the camp during its entire thirteen-month existence. His family lived across the street from the camp. He was about ten years old at the time. After I explained to him I was interviewing people involved with the camp and how the CPS system worked, he said, "Now they thought they should be paid. I thought this was more of an honor prison camp, but you say it wasn't." He then went on to share his memories of the camp from his childhood.

"The men could out-talk and out-debate anyone. They were well-educated and good-natured. Some of them were lawyers. They played games. Dad thought it was all a big joke.

"He gave them crosscut saws to cut down trees. A crosscut saw requires two men, one on each handle. There's quite an act to running a crosscut saw. If Dad wasn't watching, they wasted time. They'd take a block of wood and round it at the bottom like a rocking chair. They sat on the block and rocked while holding the saw. They spent more time making the rocking chair block than they did cutting trees. If it weren't for the foremen cutting firewood for them, they would have frozen to death.

"If the temperature was below 0 degrees, they were not required to work outside. They rigged the thermometer somehow to read below 0 degrees most mornings. They fooled the camp manager for a while with that one.

"Harvey Saunders, Dad's boss, didn't take their jokes as well as the younger men. Harvey spoke with a broken accent and was respected for being a good man in the woods. They got a kick out of playing games on him. When they went to cut firewood for the winter, the saws and axes would be missing. Harvey was fit to be tied; he didn't know what to do. All of a sudden, the tools would be back in their proper place. They didn't steal things; they just played games.

"They let me ride my bike through their dorm. My bike broke and they fixed it. One day, a cow strayed into the camp. One of the men put a rope around its neck and led it into the dorm where it let some cow pies drop (fly). Instead of cleaning it up, they made a 'Detour' sign on a stick and placed it in the cow pie. They just walked around it. They made jokes out of anything.

"The local people didn't like them because their boys were in the service getting shot at and these men wouldn't go. People really frowned on them. Owners of the local grocery stores wouldn't sell them groceries or the local people would stop patronizing that store.

"Someone drove them into Manistique or Newberry once a week for recreation. As soon as the people found out who they were, they'd put the run on them and they'd hightail it back to Germfask. Because they had so much trouble outside camp, someone came to camp once a week to show a movie. We kids went to camp and watched it with them. One time, my sister [Roana] started crying during a sad movie. One of the men came over and said, 'Don't worry; it's all wrapped up in that reel back there.'

They were good-hearted people, but they'd do anything to make sure work didn't get done.

"Dad became good friends with one man who taught my sister piano lessons. He came to our house often."

RAONA MACAULAY

Max Macaulay's sister

May 2005 Interview

"They outsmarted everybody, made fools out of the people working there.

"One CO, Besinger, gave me piano lessons. His glasses were so thick he would have never been accepted into the army. He was very kind and enjoyed teaching me. He lent me his music magazines; I didn't know there was anything like those magazines. He played really well. After my lesson, my mom would say, 'Do you have a few minutes to play the piano for us?' He played classical, jazz, blues, pop, everything, without any music to read. He was so talented.

"The men in the camp were young to fifty or sixty years old. One was adept at unlocking locks. The buildings and vehicles were locked every night, and every morning everything was unlocked. It was a joke they played on the workers. They never took anything; they just undid all the locks. The post office had a big safe. The postmaster forgot the combination. He had a CO open it for him. After it was done, he said, 'Now just forget the combination.'

"If the men had good behavior, they could go to Manistique. They were met with eggs and rotten produce.

"They were lawyers, well-educated; they could out-talk and out-debate anyone."

OMAR DORAN

2005 Interview

Omar Doran, a lifelong resident of Germfask, being interviewed in 2005 by Marcus Rosenbaum of National Public Radio.

Author's photo

"I was a very young boy at the time the camp was here. When the COs walked down the street, we young boys and not so young boys threw snowballs or stones at them along with verbal insults that I will not repeat here. We were only repeating what the adults were saying; I was too young to really know what was going on.

"They never once made any remark to insult us, nor did they make any physical moves that gave any indication they might hurt us, never. They would pull their jackets over their heads for protection, smile at us, and keep walking. They suffered the indignity and kept on going.

"When they rode into town, people would throw eggs at them.

"I don't remember any of them being rich, but I do remember they were all educated and able to solve any problem. They all seemed to have a trade. I remember a combination lock at the post office was either lost or broken, and a CO was asked to open it. We watched as he worked the lock, and sure enough, he got it open without breaking it.

"Some of the farmers would throw verbal abuses one day and ask for their help the following day. They were always available and willing to help the farmers repair machinery. Whenever you needed help, they were there.

"I guess they figured they'd win if they stuck it out long enough.

"A lot of people in town thought the COs had life too easy. Most families did not have indoor plumbing, but the camp had perhaps twenty stalls and showers. The people thought the government was giving them more than they had. The indoor plumbing caused hard feelings. Most people thought they should have less than the local people, and that they should be out doing hard labor every day, breaking rocks with a pickaxe.

"The Mennonite church really suffered and Bruce Handrich had a difficult time. As late as the 1960s, people still associated him with that camp. They either ignored or insulted him. That's all changed now, of course. He is probably the most respected person in the area.

"When I think of the Germfask COs today, I compare them to the Japanese Americans who were put into 'protective custody' during World War II. They did suffer here, but they suffered with dignity."

GERMFASK TODAY

The Seney National Wildlife Headquarters, just north of Germfask on highway M77, is a travel destination to thousands of people annually, but the town they drive through to get there, Germfask, usually goes unnoticed. It's one of those small villages whose population has dwindled, leaving many unused and boarded-up former businesses. The elementary school closed in 1988 and the children are now bused to Manistique. The residents turned the vacated school into an active community center. Five churches, Kersh's General Store, two canoe rentals and campsites on the banks of the Manistique River, the Jolly Inn Bar, and a motel still remain.

Who, driving through, would suspect he was passing a World War II center for protest? A sign on the roadside marks the site of the former CCC camp, located on the banks of the Manistique River, but the date is incorrect. The CCC men left in 1942 and the buildings remained vacant until the conscientious objectors arrived in 1944 and transferred out in 1945.

Today the former CCC camp is the site of Big Cedar Campground and Livery.

Only the sidewalks remain

When the camp closed, the government allowed the dorms to be moved from the site. The Zellar family of Germfask converted one into a house to raise their eleven children.

Ironically, two dorms were moved to Manistique and are owned and used by the Veterans of Foreign Wars (VFW). The veterans placed panel-ing over the interior walls many years ago. If the paneling were removed, the carvings the COs made in the wooden walls would be visible. The present veterans are aware of the buildings' history.

The Jolly Inn Bar and Restaurant is still a thriving business owned by the Tovey Family, fifth generation descendants of the Grant family. (Grant is the G in Germfask.)

It's known for its cleanliness and home-cooked meals. Someone driving through wouldn't give it a second glance but on summer evenings, the locals wait for a table, and while waiting, they sit at the same bar the conscientious objectors did in 1944.

APPENDIXES

APPENDIX A: LIST OF 151 CPS CAMPS[23]

CIVILIAN PUBLIC SERVICE CAMPS

No.	Tech. Agency	Operat. Group	Location	Open. Date	Clos. Date
A	SCS	AFSC	Richmond, Ind.	June '41	July '41
1	FS	BSC	Manistee, Mich.	June '41	July '41
2	FS	AFSC	San Dimas, Calif.	June '41	Dec. '42
3	NPS	AFSC	Patapsco, Md.	May '41	Sept. '42
4	SCS	MCC	Grottoes, Va.	May '41	May '46
5	SCS	MCC	Colorado Springs, Colo.	June '41	May '46
6	SCS	BSC	Lagro, Ind.	May '41	Nov. '44
7	SCS	BSC	Magnolia, Ark.	June '41	Nov. '44
8	FS	MCC	Marietta, Ohio	June '41	Apr. '43
9	FS	AFSC	Petersham, Mass.	June '41	Oct. '42
10	FS	AFSC	Royalston, Mass.	June '41	Oct. '42
11	FS	AFSC	Ashburnham, Mass.	June '41	Oct. '42
12	FS	AFSC	Cooperstown, N.Y.	June '41	May '45
13	FS	MCC	Bluffton, Ind.	June '41	Mar. '42
14	SCS	AFSC	Merom, Ind.	June '41	Apr. '43
15	FS	ACCO	Stoddard, N.H.	Aug. '41	Oct. '42
16	FS	BSC	Kane, Pa.	July '41	Nov. '44
17	FS	BSC	Stronach, Mich.	Aug. '41	June '42
18	SCS	MCC	Denison, Iowa	Aug. '41	Sept. '46
19	NPS	AFSC	Buck Creek, N.C.	Aug. '41	May '43
20	SCS	MCC	Wells Tannery, Pa.	Oct. '41	Oct. '44
21	FS	BSC	Cascade Locks, Ore.	Nov. '41	July '46
22	SCS	MCC	Henry, Ill.	Nov. '41	Nov. '42
23	SCS	AFSC	Coshocton, Ohio	Jan. '42	Feb. '46
24	SCS	MCC	(1) Hagerstown, Md.	Feb. '42	Sept. '46
		BSC	(2) Williamsport, Md.		
		MCC	(3) Boonsboro, Md.		
		MCC	(4) Clearspring, Md.		
		BSC	(5) New Windsor, Md.		
25	SCS	MCC	Weeping Water, Nebr.	Apr. '42	Apr. '43
26	GH	ACCO	Chicago, Ill.	Mar. '42	July '46
27	PHS	BSC	(1) Tallahassee, Fla.	Mar. '42	
		MCC	(2) Mulberry, Fla. & Bartow, Fla.		Dec. '46
		AFSC	(3) Orlando, Fla.		
		BSC	(4) Gainesville, Fla.		
28	FS	MCC	Medaryville, Ind.	Apr. '42	May '46
29	FS	BSC	Lyndhurst, Va.	May '42	Jan. '44
30	FS	BSC	Walhalla, Mich.	May '42	Nov. '43
31	FS	MCC	Camino, Calif.	Apr. '42	Dec. '46
32	FS	AFSC	Campton, N.H.	May '42	Nov. '43
33	SCS	MCC	Fort Collins, Colo.	June '42	Oct. '46
34	F&W	*BSC	Buckingham Side Camp Bowie, Md.	June '42	
34-D.S.			Detached Service		
35	FS	MCC	North Fork, Calif.	May '42	Mar. '46
36	FS	BSC	Santa Barbara, Calif.	June '42	Apr. '44
37	FS	*AFSC	Coleville, Calif.	June '42	Mar. '46
38	Hosp.	BSC	Salem, Ore.	Not opened	
39	NPS	MCC	Galax, Va.	June '42	Mar. '43
40	SCS	MCC	Howard, Pa.	June '42	June '43
41	MH	*AFSC	Williamsburg, Va.	June '42	July '46
42	FS	BSC	Wellston, Mich.	June '42	Sept. '46

23   National Interreligious Service Board for Conscientious Objectors, *Directory of Civilian Public Service,* Washington, D.C.

CIVILIAN PUBLIC SERVICE CAMPS

No.	Tech. Agency	Operat. Group	Location	Open. Date	Clos. Date
43	PRRA	BSC	Castaner Project Adjuntas, Puerto Rico	July '42	
		MCC	Aibonita, P.R.		
		AFSC	Zalduondo, P.R.		
		BSC	St. Thomas, Virgin Islands		
44	MH	MCC	Staunton, Va.	Aug. '42	Sept. '46
45	NPS	MCC	Luray, Va.	Aug. '42	July '46
46	SCS	*AFSC	Big Flats, N.Y.	Aug. '42	Oct. '46
47	MH	BSC	Sykesville, Md.	Aug. '42	July '46
48	FS	BSC	Marienville, Pa.	Oct. '42	Nov. '43
49	MH	*AFSC	Philadelphia, Pa.	Aug. '42	Oct. '46
50	MH	AFSC	New York, N.Y.	Sept. '42	Jan. '46
51	MH	BSC	Ft. Steilacoom, Wash.	Sept. '42	Oct. '45
52	SCS	AFSC-MCC	Powellsville, Md.	Oct. '42	
53	FS	AFSC	Gorham, N.H.	Oct. '42	Apr. '43
54	FS	ACCO	Warner, N.H.	Oct. '42	Feb. '43
55	NPS	MCC	Belton, Mont.	Sept. '42	Oct. '46
56	FS	BSC	Waldport, Ore.	Oct. '42	Apr. '46
57	BR	MCC	Hill City, S. Dak.	Oct. '42	May '46
58	MH	MCC	Farnhurst, Dela.	Nov. '42	Oct. '46
59	GLO	AFSC	Elkton, Ore.	Nov. '42	Feb. '46
60	BR	MCC	Lapine, Ore.	Dec. '42	Jan. '43
61	GH	MCWP	Durham, N.C.	Dec. '42	Oct. '46
62	TS	*AFSC	Cheltenham, Md.	Dec. '42	Apr. '46
63	MH	MCC	Marlboro, N.J.	Nov. '42	Oct. '46
64	FSA	MCC	Terry, Mont.	Jan. '43	July '46
65	MH		Utica, N.Y.	Not opened	
66	MH	MCC	Norristown, Pa.	Dec. '42	Oct. '46
67	SCS	MCC	Downey, Idaho	Nov. '42	Feb. '46
68	MH	BSC	Norwich, Conn.	Mar. '43	Aug. '46
69	MH	AFSC-MCC	Cleveland, Ohio	Dec. '42	Oct. '46
70	MH	BSC	Dayton, Ohio	Oct. '43	June '46
71	MH	MCC	Lima, Ohio	Jan. '43	Sept. '46
72	MH	MCC	Macedonia, Ohio	Dec. '42	Sept. '46
73	MH	BSC	Columbus, Ohio	Dec. '42	June '46
74	MH	BSC	Cambridge, Md.	Dec. '42	July '46
75	MH	AFSC	Medical Lake, Wash.	Feb. '43	May '45
76	FS	*AFSC	Glendora, Calif.	Jan. '43	Dec. '46
77	MH	MCC	Greystone Park, N.J.	Jan. '43	Aug. '46
78	MH	MCC	Denver, Colo.	Jan. '43	Mar. '46
79	MH	MCC	Provo, Utah	Mar. '43	Apr. '46
80	MH	BSC	Lyons, N.J.	Apr. '43	Aug. '46
81	MH	*AFSC	Middletown, Conn.	Mar. '43	Sept. '46
82	MH	BSC	Newtown, Conn.	Mar. '43	Sept. '46
83	MH	*AFSC	Warren, Pa.	Feb. '43	May '46
84	MH	*AFSC	Concord, N.H.	Feb. '43	June '46
85	MH	MCC	Howard, R.I.	Feb. '43	Oct. '46
86	MH	MCC	Mt. Pleasant, Iowa	Feb. '43	Sept. '46
87	MH	*AFSC	Brattleboro, Vt.	Feb. '43	Sept. '46
88	MH	BSC	Augusta, Maine	Apr. '43	May '46
89	FS	AFSC	Oakland, Md.	Mar. '43	Apr. '43
90	MH	MCC	Ypsilanti, Mich.	Mar. '43	Oct. '46
91	MH	BSC	Mansfield, Conn.	Mar. '43	Aug. '46
92	TS	MCC	Vineland, N.J.	Apr. '43	June '46
93	MH	MCC	Harrisburg, Pa.	Apr. '43	Aug. '46
94	FSA	*AFSC	Trenton, N. Dak.	Apr. '43	Mar. '46
95	TS	BSC	Buckley, Wash.	May '43	Oct. '45
96	MH	MCC	Rochester, Minn.		

CIVILIAN PUBLIC SERVICE CAMPS

No.	Tech. Agency	Operat. Group	Location	Open. Date	Clos. Date
97 & 100	ALA	AFSC-BSC-MCC (BSC)	Dairy Farm and Dairy Herd Tester Proj.	May '43	Oct. '46
			Oneida, N.Y.		
			King Co., Wash.		
			Coos Co., Ore.		
			Elgin, Ill.		
			New Windsor, Md.		
		(MCC)	Colorado Area		
			Penna. and Md. Area		
			Mich. and Ohio Area		
			New England Area		
			Pacific Coast Area		
			Wisconsin Area		
			Iowa Area		
			Maine Area		
		(AFSC)	Eastern Area		
98	C&GS	SSS	Coast & Geodetic Survey	May '43	Sept. '46
99	FS&R	AFSC	Chungking, China	May '43	Oct. '43
100	(See No. 97)				
101	DS	NSBRO	Foreign Relief & Rehabilitation Proj., Philadelphia, Pa.	May '43	Oct. '43
102	TS	*ACCO	Rosewood, Owings Mills, Md.	May '43	July '46
103	FS	MCC	Missoula, Mont.	May '43	Apr. '46
104	AES	*AFSC	Ames, Iowa	May '43	May '46
105	MH	BSC	Lynchburg, Colony, Va.	May '43	Apr. '46
106	AES	MCC	Lincoln—No. Platte, Nebr.	May '43	Oct. '46
107	NPS	MCC	Three Rivers, Calif.	May '43	June '46
108	NPS	*AFSC	Gatlinburg, Tennessee	June '43	Dec. '46
109	MH	BSC	Marion, Va.	June '43	June '46
110	MH	MCC	Allentown, Pa.	Nov. '43	May '46
111	BR	SSS	Mancos, Colo.	July '43	Feb. '46
112	AES	BSC	East Lansing, Mich.	July '43	Apr. '46
113	AES	BSC	Duluth, Grand Rapids, St. Paul & Waseca, Minn.	Aug. '43	Aug. '46
114	WB	BSC	Mt. Weather, Bluemont, Va.	Sept. '43	June '46
115	OSRD	AFSC-[BSC-MCC	Office of Scientific Research & Development	Oct. '43	Oct. '46
116	AES	BSC	College Park, Md.	Sept. '43	Sept. '46
117	TS	MCC	Lafayette, R. I.	Nov. '43	Aug. '46
118	MH	MCC	Wernersville, Pa.	Nov. '43	June '46
119	TS	*AFSC	New Lisbon, N.J.	Dec. '43	Oct. '46
120	MH	MCC	Kalamazoo, Mich.	Dec. '43	July '46
121	NPS	BSC	Bedford, Va.	Feb. '44	June '46
122	MH	MCC	Winnebago, Wisc.	Dec. '43	Mar. '46
123	TS	MCC	Union Grove, Wisc.	Dec. '43	July '46
124	TS	*AFSC	Stockley, Dela.	Dec. '43	Sept. '46
125	AES	MCC	Orono, Maine	Dec. '43	May '46
126	USDA	MCC	Beltsville, Md.	Feb. '44	Dec. '46
127	TS	MCC	American Fork, Utah	Jan. '44	Feb. '46
128	BR	SSS	Lapine, Ore.	Jan. '44	Dec. '46
129	MH	*AFSC	Pennhurst, Spring City, Pa.	Jan. '44	Aug. '46
130	TS	*AFSC	Pownal, Maine	Feb. '44	July '46
131	MH	MCWP	Cherokee, Iowa	Feb. '44	May '46
132	TS	*AFSC	Laurel, Md.	Feb. '44	July '46
133	AES	*AFSC	Wooster, Ohio	Mar. '44	Apri '46
134	FS	BSC	Belden, Calif.	May '44	May '46
135	F&W	SSS	Germfask, Mich.	May '44	June '45
136	MH	*ABHMS	Skillman, N.J.	July '44	Oct. '46
137	MH	Ev.&Ref.	Independence, Iowa	Dec. '44	Sept. '46

138	SCS	MCC	(1) Lincoln, Nebr.	Oct. '44	Dec. '46
			(2) Malcolm, Nebr.		
			(3) Waterloo, Nebr.		Apr. '46
139	MH	Disc. of Chr.	Logansport, Ind.	Oct. '44	Apr. '46
140	OSG	AFSC-BSC	Army Epidemiological Board	Feb. '45	Oct. '46
141	PHS	MCC	Gulfport, Miss.	Feb. '45	Not closing
142	MH	MCC	Woodbine, N.J.	Jan. '45	July '46
143	MH	MCC	Catonsville, Md.	Feb. '45	Aug. '46
144	MH	MCC	Poughkeepsie, N.Y.	Apr. '45	Apr. '46
145	TS	MCC	Wassiac, N.Y.		
146	AES	BSC	Ithaca, N.C.	July '45	June '46
147	MH	MCC	Tiffin, Ohio	June '45	Nov. '45
148	FS	SSS	Minersville, Calif.	June '45	Dec. '46
149	FS	AFSC-BSC	U.S. Forest Service Research Proj.	June '45	June '46
150	MH	MCC	Livermore, Calif.	Nov. '45	Dec. '46
151	MH	MCC	Roseburg, Ore.	Dec. '45	Dec. '46

Legend

*	Taken over by Government before unit closed
ABHMS	American Baptist Home Mission Society
ACCO	Association of Catholic Conscientious Objectors
AES	Agriculture Experiment Station
AFSC	American Friends Service Committee
ALA	Agriculture Experiment Station
BR	Bureau of Reclamation
BSC	Brethren Service Committee
C&GS	Coast & Goedetic Survey
Dis. Chr.	Disciples of Christ
E&R	Evangelical & Reformed
F&W	Fish & Wild Life
FS	Forest Service
FS&R	Foreign Service & Relief
FSA	Farm Security Administration
GH	General Hospital
GLO	General Land Office
MCC	Mennonite Central Committee
MCWP	Methodist Commission on World Peace
MH	Mental Hospital
NPS	National Park Service
NSBRO	National Service Board for Religious Objectors
OSG	Office of Surgeon General
OSBD	Office of Scientific Research & Development
PHS	Public Health Service
PRRA	Puerto Rican Reconstruction Administration
SCS	Soil Conservation Service
SSS	Selective Service System
TS	Training School
WB	Weather Bureau

APPENDIX B: LIST OF GERMFASK CONSCIENTIOUS OBJECTORS

From Mennonite Central Committee

Andresen, Bent B.	Baird, George H.	Banaszak, Ernest	Bankert, Wallace A.
Beck, Vincent S.	Bell, Morris A.	Besinger, Curtis	Beyreis, Louis J.
Bishop, Corbett	Bode, Arden D.	Borglund, Robert .	Bose, Clement
Bradshaw, Henry S.	Brainerd, Robert S.	Calef, John H.	Carpenter, Joseph
Chester, John F.	Cimbanin, Michael A.	Coffman, John S.	Cole, George
Cole, Roger W.	Collier, Eugene Emerson	Cook, Marvin H.	Cordell, Robert J.
Crowder, Paul C.	Cullen, Raymond K.	Culler, A. Dwight	Daniel, Homer L.
De Voute, John	DeVault, Don C.	Dingman, Daniel	Dingman, Gerald F.
Evans, Lyonell K.	Fell, George B.	Fiore, Pasquale P.	Flincker, Harold R.
Flowers, Dewey W.	Gadol, Sol	Galbraith, Douglas	Goudy, William C.
Guckemus, Philip	Hall, Andrew A.	Hatfield, Frank W.	Hawkins, Richard E.
Haynes, Wells J.	Hoehn, Maurice S.	Hogenauer, Irwin	Hood, Jack
Hopkins, Jason J.	Hordinski, Bill W.		
Horowitz, Morris	Hughes, Warren Y.	Jenkins, Osley	Kauble, John H.
Kehl, Christian H.	Kekoni, Leo A.	Kepler, Roy C	Key, Norman
Kirk, Donald E.	Kruger, Ernest W.	Lang, Clifford L.	Lawson, Norman
Lazarus, Richard C.	Lehmann, Arthur	Lewis, Leonard W.	Love, John
Lupo, C. Fred	Martin, Joseph L.	Mattox, Charles M. J.	Meneyes, John
Migliorino, Nicholas	Miller, David J.	Mitaraky, John	Mitchell, Donald
Mullen, Charles	Ness, Walter	Neubrand, John K.	Neumann, William
Nichols, George H.	Olson, Karl E.	Plant, Alvin	Pope, Calvin C.
Pulliam, Ralph E.	Riddle, Iredell R.	Riddles, James A.	Robutka, Walter
Scantlen, Robert E.	Shattuck, Claude R.	Smith, Harvey S.	Stokes, John S.
Stoll, John F.	Strang, Lloyd A.	Tavernier, William E.	Taylor, Hollen W.
Teague, Philip E.	Tiebe, Charles E.	Truempelman, Arthur William	Watkins, Harry J.
Wesner, Ervin	Wright, Millard L.	Yamada, George H.	Yoder, Carl Quinten

APPENDIX C: CONSCIENTIOUS OBJECTORS—IN RETROSPECT

Approximately 500 conscientious objectors who volunteered to become human guinea pigs made valuable contributions toward improving the living conditions of mankind. Information gained from the Keys medical starvation experiment, Salk's polio research, and other medical guinea pig experiments, is used today to treat many illnesses, including mass starvation in underdeveloped countries.

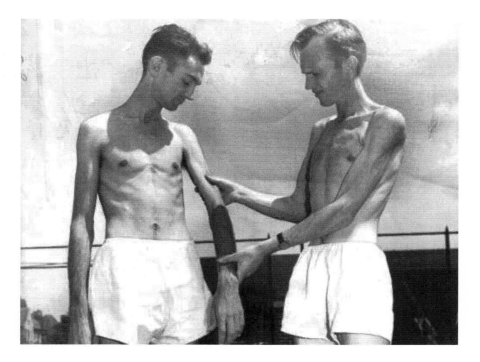

Conscientious objectors who were voluntary participants in Dr. Ancel Keys' medical starvation experiment at the University of Minnesota between November 19, 1944 and December 20, 1945. The images on this page are credited to the Hennepin County Libraries Special Collections.

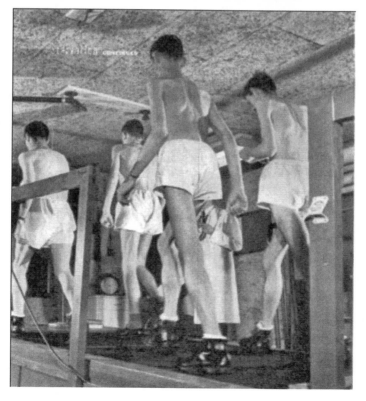

Conscientious objectors who worked in mental institutions wrote letters and complained about the inhumane treatment of patients. Their letters and complaints prompted *Life* magazine to write an article exposing those conditions, and as a result, legislation was passed to correct these problems and others.

The smokejumpers began July 12, 1940, as an experiment that lasted through 1943 when it became an official branch of the U.S. Forest Service. Because of the wartime man shortage, the majority of men used to refine this project were recruited from Civilian Public Service. Major William Cary Lee of the U.S. Army adapted the parachuting techniques learned by the Forest Service to train the army's first paratroop group at Fort Benning, Georgia, which was later used by the 101st Airborne Division during the Normandy invasion.

In 1947, the Friends Service Council (Quakers) was the recipient of the Nobel Peace Prize in recognition both for pioneering work in the international peace movement and of humanitarian work carried out without regard for race or nationality.

APPENDIX D: CPS PROTEST SONGS

Songs campers composed and sang at meals

Time: March, April, and May of 1944

Place: CPS camps: Mancos, Colorado, and La Pine, Oregon

WAY DOWN UPON THE DESCHUTES RIVER

Tune: Swanee River

By Al Partridge

Way down upon the Deschutes River

Far, far, away

That's where the c.o.s do slave labor

Working without no pay.

Chorus

All the camp is sad and weary,

Listen to our moan.

Oh, Hershey, how our hearts grow weary,

Sponging on the old folks at home.

We're working for the Reclamation,

Nine hours a day.

But we don't get no compensation,

Lord, we don't get no pay.

Chorus

I'VE BEEN WORKING IN THE TIMBER

Tune: Working on Railroad

Composed by Tiny, a CO

I've been working in the timber,

All the live-long day.

I've been working in the timber

But I don't get any pay.

Can't you hear those bells a ringing?

Rise up so early in the morn?

"Tiny, blow your horn."

OPPOSITION TO CONSCRIPTION

Tune: Love of Jesus

I've got the opposition to conscription,

Down in my heart,

Down in my heart,

Down in my heart.

Repeat above and then add, "to stay."

I know that Hershey doesn't like it,

But it's down in my heart,

Down in my heart.

Again repeat above and add, "to stay."

KILL, KILL, KILL
Tune Old Black Joe
By Frank Hatfield

Gone are the days when I had my liberty,
I am a slave in the country of the free.
Gone are the truths that now I cling to still,
I hear once gentle voices shouting, "Kill, kill, kill!"
Chorus:
Conscription, constriction, it takes away man's will.
And bows his soul to voices shouting, "Kill, kill, kill!"

4F AND S. Q. SONG
By Frank Hatfield
The "Murch" referred to was the camp director

The Dr. pulled my teeth all out.
He found my heart was bad.
He looked at me and said "T.B.,"
and even thought me <u>mad.</u>

Chorus:
Oh, get those 4Fs through, Murch.
Get those 4Fs through.
For I've been here for half a year
and always been S.Q.

"Now boys don't get impatient,"
our layman doctor said.
But I'm so weak, my bones do creak,
and I can't get out of bed.

Chorus

"Now boys, while you are waiting,
you cannot go S.Q.
so do light work or else, you jerk,
it's R.T.W.

Chorus

Now rigor mortis has set in,
my bones are stiff and cold,
I have gangrene, as all have seen,
yet I'm not sick, I'm told.

Chorus

And that's the way it goes, boys
that's just what he said,
so rest in peace, for your release,
will come when you are dead.

Chorus

Last Chorus
Oh, get those coffins made, Murch,
get those coffins made
For I'm not strong, I've not got long
before I will be dead.

CONSCRIPTION BILL

Tune: Jesse James' Death

It was on a Sat. night
and the moon was shining bright,
when they passed that conscription bill.
And for miles and miles away
you could hear the people say,
"Twas the Pres. and boys on Capitol Hill."

Chorus:

Oh, Franklin Roosevelt told the people how he felt,
and they darned near believed what he said.
He said, "I hate war and so does Eleanor,
but we won't be safe 'til everybody's dead."

When my dear old mother died,
I was sitting by her side,
and I promised her to war I'd never go.
Now I'm wearing khaki jeans,
and eating army beans,
and I'm told J.P. Morgan loves me so.

Chorus

THE CO BLUES

(Tune St. Louis Blues)

I've got these CO blues,

I'm just as blue as blue can be.

It's all because, it's all because,

It's all because of what Selective Service did to me.

I signed old form 47, conscientiously you see,

Now see what Selective Service has done to me.

They told me the work would be good,

They sent me out to the woods,

And all I do,

Is cut notches in the trees.

Cut notches until I'm down on my knees.

And when it's 28 below,

Oh, Lord how I do freeze.

I'm getting bluer every day,

And I don't know how long it will be,

But the man who signs my release,

Before I get out of this mess,

The Lord will surely bless?

MONEY PAY-TRIOTS

(Tune: Clementine)

Join the party that is ruling

Give the boss what brains you've got

Play the rooster, be a booster;

And you'll be a patriot.

   Chorus

O, my country, O, my country,

How I love each blooming spot,

But ain't it funny how for money

One may be a patriot.

Go to church, and talk like honey,

Kiss the flay, and shout a lot,

That will make you, for they'll take you

For a blooming patriot.

Boom your business, boom your business,

Brother love it matters not.

Use your gall, sir, do them all, sir,

Then you'll be a patriot.

** ("Money Pay-trots" attempts to reveal the usual Fourth-of-July type of "patriotic spouting" for what it is – money grabbing and hypocritical expressions of belief in Christianity and devotion to one's country.)

OUR OLD AND DUSTY LOAN

Oh the bad boys gone

From the forests of La Pine,

They've left for a camp in Michigan

The Director thinks all the brains have gone with them,

But we'll carry on the work the "Slobs" began.

So weep no more for Mancos,

The brains are not all gone

We will sing this song

To our friends so far away

And the fight which they began,

Carry On!

THE SELECTIVE SERVICE ARTILLERY

(Tune: The Caissons Go Rolling Along

Olsen was the Administrator of CPS camps

Over hill, over dale

COs moan without avail

As Old Olsen goes marching along,

Laws are smashed, rules are mashed,

And democracy is bashed,

As Old Olsen goes scheming along.

COs work all the day

But they sure don't get the pay

Like Old Olsen who marches along,

Hershey bars all around

Keeps us guys from going to town

But Old Olsen goes traipsing along.

CHORUS

So it's work, work, work

You poor, old CO jerk

Fighting for liberty

Civilian Public Service

Makes everybody nervous

But Old Olsen from Washington, D.C.

AMERICA THE BEAUTIFUL

(Here is another type of patriotism –
wider and more meaningful.)

O beautiful for spacious skies,

For amber waves of grain,

For purple mountain majesties

Above the fruited plain,

America, America,

God shed his grace on thee,

And crown thy good with brotherhood

From sea to shining sea.

O beautiful for pilgrim feet,

Whose stern, impassioned stress

A thoroughfare for freedom beat

Across the wilderness,

America, America

God mend thine every flaw,

Confirm thy soul in self-control

Thy liberty in law.

I KNOW THAT CONSCRIPTION IS WRONG

(Tune: I'm going down the road feeling bad)

I'm here but, I know that conscription is wrong,

I'm here but, I know that conscription is wrong,

I'm here but, I know conscription is wrong,

Lord, Lord, I ain't gonna be treated this way.

I'm working for ten cents a day, I'm working for ten cents a day,

Lord, Lord, I ain't gonna be treated this way.

I'm going down the road feeling bad.

I'm going down the road feeling bad.

I'm going down the road feeling bad.

Lord, Lord, I ain't gonna be treated this way.

MY COUNTRY IS THE WORLD

(Tune: America)

(Only when a country is free and independent can it take its place in the world community)

My country is the world;

My flag with stars impearled,

Fills all the skies.

All the round earth I claim,

People of every name,

My heart would prize.

And all men are my kin,

Since every man has been

Blood of my blood;

I glory in the grace

And strength of every race,

And joy in every trace

Of brotherhood.

CHRISTIANS AT WAR

TUNE: Onward Christian Soldiers

Onward, Christian soldiers! Duty's way is plain;

Slay your Christian neighbors, or by them be slain.

Puppeteers are spouting effervescent swill,

God above is calling you to rob and rape and kill,

All your acts are sanctified by the Lamb on high;

If you love the Holy Ghost, go murder, pray, and die.

Onward, Christian soldiers, rip and tear and smite!

Let the gentle Jesus bless your dynamite.

Splinter skulls with shrapnel, fertilize the sod;

Folks who do not speak your tongue deserve the curse of God.

Smash the doors of every home, pretty maidens seize;

Use your might and sacred right to treat them as you please.

Onward, Christian soldiers! Eat and drink and fill;

Rob the bloody fingers, Christ O.K.'s the bill.

Steal the farmer's savings, take their grain and meat;

Even though the children starve, the Savior's bums must eat.

Burn the peasant's cottage, orphans leave bereft;

In Jehovah's holy name, wreak ruin right and left.

Onward, Christian soldiers! Drench the land with gore;

Mercy is a weakness all the gods abhor.

Bayonet the babies jab the mothers, too;

Host the cross of Calvary to hallow all you do.

File the bullets' noses flat, poison every well,

God decrees your enemies must all go plum to hell.

Onward, Christian soldiers! Lighting all you meet,

Trampling human freedom under pious feet.

Praise the Lord whose dollar sign dupes his favored race!

Trust in mock salvation, serve as pirates' tools,

History will say of you, "That pack of G—d fools."

BIBLIOGRAPHY

BOOKS

Anderson, Jervis. *Bayard Rustin: Troubles I've Seen*. New York: HarperCollins, 1997.

Cornell, Julien. *The Conscientious Objector and the Law*. New York, NY: Jerome S. Ozer, 1972.

Cowan, Sam K. *Sergeant York and His People*. New York, NY: Grosset & Dunlap, 1922.

Crowe, William S. *Lumberjack: Inside an Era in the Upper Peninsula of Michigan. 1952*. 50th Anniversary ed. Eds. Lynn McGlothlin Emerick and Ann McGlothlin Weller. Skandia, MI: North Country Publishing, 2002.

French, Paul Comly. *We Won't Murder: The History of Non-Violence*. NY: Hastings House, 1940.

Gandhi, M. K. *Gandhi Autobiography*. Trans. Mahadeu Desai. Washington, DC: Public Affairs Press, 1948.

Gandhi, Mahatma. *The Essential Gandhi*. Vol. 2. 2nd ed. Ed. Louis Fisher. New York: Vintage Books, 2002.

Germfask: Michigan Centennial, 1866-1966. Germfask, MI: Germfask Centennial Committee, 1966.

Hershberger, Guy Franklin. *War, Peace & Nonresistance*. Scottdale, PA: Herald Press, 1944.

Hershberger, Guy Franklin. *The Mennonite Church in the Second World War*. Scottdale, PA: Mennonite Publishing House, 1951.

Holbrook, Stewart H. *Holy Old Mackinaw: A Natural History of the American Lumberjack*. New York, NY: The Macmillan Company, 1948.

Jacob, Philip Ernest. *The Origins of Civilian Public Service*. Washington, D.C..: National Service Board for Religious Objectors, 1941.

Keim, Albert N. *The CPS Story: An Illustrated History of Civilian Public Service*. Intercourse, PA: Good Books, 1990.

Kramer, Ann. *Refusing to Fight: Conscientious Objectors of the Second World War*. South Yorkshire, Gr. Brit.: Pen & Sword Books, 2013.

Krehbiel, Nicholas A. *General Lewis B. Hershey and Conscientious Objection During World War II*. Columbia, MO: U of Missouri P, 2011.

LeDuc, Vonciel M. *Manistique*. Chicago, IL: Arcadia Publishing, 2009.

Leuchtenburg, William D. *Franklin D. Roosevelt and the New Deal*. New York: Harper Row, 1963.

Losey, Elizabeth. *Seney National Wildlife Refuge: Its Story*. Marquette, MI: Lake Superior Press, 2003.

McQuiddy, Steve. *Here on the Edge: How a Small Group of World War II Conscientious Objectors Took Art and Peace from the Margins to the Mainstream*. Corvallis, OR: Oregon State UP, 2013.

Morrison, Roger. *When the Farmers Came to Seney*. Pickford, MI, 1982.

Moskos, Charles C. edited by Chambers II. John Whiteclay,. *The New Conscientious Objection from Sacred to Secular Resistance*. Oxford, Gr. Brit.: Oxford UP, 1993.

National Interreligious Service Board for Conscientious Objectors. *Directory of CPS*. Scottdale, PA: 1996.

National Interreligious Service Board for Conscientious Objectors. *The Origins of Civilian Public Service*. Washington, DC. No date listed.

Pyle, Ernie. *Brave Men*. New York, NY: Grosset & Dunlap, 1943.

Prater, Rosella. *Mennonite Stirrings in "America's Playland."* Nappanee, IN: Evangel Press, 1987.

Reimann, Lewis C. *Incredible Seney*. AuTrain, MI: Avery Color Studios, 1982.

Remarque, Erich Maria. *All Quiet on the Western Front*. trans. A. W. Wheen. Boston, MA: Little Brown and Company, 1929.

Riordan, John J. *The Dark Peninsula: A Tale About Life in Michigan's Upper Peninsula in the Days When White Pine Was King*. AuTrain, MI: Avery Color Studios, 1976.

Rustin, Bayard. *I Must Resist*. Ed. Michael G. Long. San Francisco: City Lights Books, 2012.

Sawyer, Alvah L. *A History of the Northern Peninsula of Michigan and Its People*. Chicago, IL: The Lewis Publishing Company, 1911.

Selective Service System. *Conscientious Objection: Special Mono-*

graph No. 11, Vol. I. Washington, DC: Government Printing Office, 1950.

Smith, Jean Edward. *FDR.* New York: Random House, 2007.

Smolens, John. *Wolf's Mouth.* East Lansing, MI: Michigan State UP, 2016.

Symon, Charles A. *We Can Do It! A History of the Civilian Conservation Corps in Michigan—1933-1941.* Gladstone, MI: RonJon Press, 1983.

Van Dyck, Harry R. *Exercise of Conscience: A WWII Objector Remembers.* Buffalo, NY: Prometheus Books, Buffalo, 1990.

FILM

Tejada-Flores, Rick and Judith Ehrlich, Dirs. *The Good War and Those Who Refused to Fight It.* Bullfrog Films, Oley, PA: Paradigm Productions.

GOVERNMENT PUBLICATIONS

Selective Service System. *Board Member Handbook.* Arlington, VA: 2007.

Selective Service System. *Selective Training and Service Act of 1940: Part 692: Rules for Government Operated Camps.* 1940.

DOCUMENTS OBTAINED THROUGH FREEDOM OF INFORMATION ACT

US Department of Justice, Washington, DC. FBI Report, Confidential Conference Regarding Closing of Camp Germfask. 2/10/1945. File number 61-11043-7.

US Department of Justice, Washington, DC. FBI Report. *Theft of Micrometer.* 7/13/1944. Findings and Conclusions. File numbers 52-27308-1 (three enclosures).

US Department of Justice, Washington, DC. FBI Report. *Alleged Insurrection and Destruction of Property.* 1/30/1945. Findings and Conclusions. File numbers 61-11043-1 (seven enclosures).

MAGAZINE ARTICLE

Eash, Sanfort. "Meet the Handrichs of Germfask." *Gospel Herald.* April 1, 1980. p. 260-261.

COURT DOCUMENTS

United States District Court. *United States v. Corbett Bishop.* No. 4956 Criminal. January 31, 1945.

United States District Court. *United States v. Corbett Bishop.* No. 4956 Criminal. February 1, 1945.

Schoolcraft County, MI Circuit Court. *People of the State of Michigan v. Marvin Cook.* January 16, 1945.

NEWSPAPERS

Manistique Pioneer Tribune (hereafter cited: *MPT*). Manistique, MI. January 3, 1911.

MPT. February 24, 1911.

MPT. January 27, 1911.

MPT. February 26, 1944.

MPT. January 18, 1945.

MPT. January 25, 1945.

MPT. January 28, 1945.

MPT. February 1, 1945

MPT. February 8, 1945.

MPT. March 15, 1945.

MPT. March 22, 1945.

MPT. April 12, 1945.

MPT. July 26, 1945.

Mining Journal Weekly. Marquette, MI. January 13, 1912.

Newberry News (hereafter cited, *NN*). Newberry, MI. March 17, 1911.

NN. March 24, 1911.

NN. April 14, 1911.

NN. April 21, 1911.

NN. December 1, 1911.

NN. January 12, 1912.

NN. July 19, 1912.

NN. October 18, 1912.

NN. January 3, 1913.

NN. January 13, 1913.

NN. July 4, 1913.

NN. December 19, 1913.

NN. March 20, 1914.

NN. July 10, 1914.

NN. December 10, 1915.

NN. December 24, 1915.

NN. February 4, 1916.

NN. February 2, 1945.

NN. February 16, 1945.

NN. March 23, 1945.

Escanaba Daily Press (hereafter cited, *EDP*). Escanaba, MI. February 3, 1945.

EDP. February 4, 1945.

EDP. February 6, 1945.

Sault Evening News. Sault St. Marie, MI. January 9, 1911.

Washington Post, (hereafter cited, *WP*). November 22, 1944.

WP. January 2, 1945.

Detroit News. January 10, 1911

Detroit Times. February 6, 1945.

ABOUT THE AUTHOR

Jane Kopecky was born and raised in Gulliver, Michigan. She is interested in local history and national political history. To further understand the government's policy toward conscientious objectors, she served for twenty years on the Selective Service draft board. This allowed her to keep abreast of present draft and pending draft laws. In addition, at each meeting, board members served as the jury in mock conscientious objector hearings.

Jane has a Master's Degree in education from Northern Michigan University and taught for many years in the Manistique Area School district before retiring.

Jane is also the author of *Huntspur and Along the Tracks*, the history of a small Upper Michigan community whose past comes to life through interviews with local residents and countless historical photographs.

You may contact Jane at janekopecky@yahoo.com.

Made in the USA
Columbia, SC
25 February 2024

32266199R00121